Behind the Badge

My Life as a Game Warden

by Dick Lang
Retired Environmental Conservation Officer

with Carol Miller
Illustrations by Vic Thibault

Richard & Gretchen Lang
4957 Hollenbeck Road
Lockport, NY 14094
716-433-7748
glang3@rochester.rr.com

I kept the names of the good guys, but changed the names of the not-so-good guys ...

Behind the Badge is available at Amazon.com in paperback, and on Kindle.

Table of Contents

4

Where Did The Last 34 Years Go?

How can this be? How can I be 71 years old and retired? I was just getting comfortable with my job! I can't be old enough to retire already!

I guess everyone feels that way when it's time to "step down." I think it was more difficult for me because I loved my job so much. In fact, it was not just my job; it was my passion, my way of life. I saw so much, learned so much, met so many great people and had so many exciting things happen to me. I have so many great stories to tell…

Introduction

As a boy growing up in the 1950s, I loved the outdoors and learned to hunt, fish, and trap from my dad. My dad and his friends were hunters and he would always let me take the first day of pheasant season off so I could walk behind him.

Dick and his father John, hunting pheasants, 1958

In 1954, I turned 14 and took the required four-hour hunter safety class at the Erie County Fairgrounds in Hamburg, NY. That was my first experience with a New York State Game Protector/Conservation Officer and I was very impressed. He caught my attention in his green uniform and his Stetson hat. And his job sounded so exciting. But, I was only a 9th grader, and who knows at that age what they want to do with their life. However, the impression stayed with me.

Dick and his father John,
hunting pheasants and rabbits, 1958

I graduated from high school in 1959 and entered the Coast Guard. Two years later, in 1961, Gretchen and I were married. By this time, I had started to think seriously about trying to get a job as a conservation officer. I told Gretchen about my dream and she encouraged me to move ahead. She has always been my biggest supporter. She introduced me to her friends, Helen and Joe Peplin. Joe was the leader of the Knapp Hill Conservation Society and promoted and taught conservation. He also encouraged me.

I took my first exam in January of 1964 and passed, but was not very high on the list. It did not matter anyway, because the list did not move. I waited and waited to be called, but nothing happened. As one of the old timers said, "The only way you get called for an interview is if someone retires or dies." While I waited, I took biology classes from the local high school and picked up classes at Buffalo State College.

Two years later another exam was held and I did much better. Then I waited again. In the meantime, I assisted Erie County 4-H Agent Walter Hallbauer with conservation projects throughout Erie County. Whenever Walt need help on a conservation project, I was there to assist. I cannot thank Walt and his wife, Gloria, enough for all their help.

Finally, on October 2, 1969, I had my interview and was appointed a New York State Conservation Officer. My first orders were simply to go to Albany and pick up my uniforms. We had no formal training in those days, there was no academy. We just learned by working with senior officers in the areas near us.

I know that my thirty-four-year career went by very fast. For the first five years I felt like a rookie, the new guy. Then came the next twenty years, the middle of my career. Then the last ten years, which I didn't know was "the end" until it happened. When I heard a sportsman say, "Lang, I heard you retired," I knew retirement was near.

I would like to thank New York State for hiring me and giving me the opportunity to work at the best job in the world, a New York State Environmental Conservation Officer.

Acknowledgements

So many people have contributed to this book.

First, my dear wife Gretchen, not just for tolerating my job, my being away at all hours of the day or night, but for being part of my life. She has inspired me in everything I've done. She has been an unpaid part of the job.

Next, my sons, their wives, and my seven grandchildren. Having all of you to share these experiences with has doubled the fun for me and made the "work" worthwhile.

Dick and Bob Osborne, Henry Haas, my brother Dave Lang, and Gary Forshee have been a part of my experiences since my childhood.

I gained so many friends over the years, other conservation officers, their families, residents of the areas where I worked, even many of the people I ticketed.

My acknowledgements could make up a book by themselves, there are so many. I hope this list is complete, but as we all know, memory plays tricks. So here goes: Don Becker, Gary Bobseine, Ron Bosela, Colin Bursey, Doug Case, Jim Groebe, Jack Hassett, Bob Kauffman, Harold Keppner, Ken Kuczka, Len Lisenbee, Frank Lohr, Morris McCargo, Alan Mills, Fred Ott, Matt Pestinger, Mike Phelps, Dennis Praczkajlo, Jim Rackl, Al Riegel, Charlie Robishaw, Jim Rogers, Neil Ross, Jeff Rupp, Dave Schultz, Dan Smoot, Jerry Sporer, Bob Sterling, Dan Sullivan, Gene Tuohey, Kimpton Vosburg, and Dan Ward.

I also acknowledge the Niagara County Sportsmen Federation and all the clubs that make up the Federation.

I want to thank outdoor writers Bill Hilts, Sr., Bill Hilts, Jr., and Will Elliot.

I coached wrestling for many years. One of my athletes, Vic Thibault, an art teacher in Newfane, NY, drew all the illustrations for the book. His work captures the stories so well that sometimes the words are superfluous.

A special thanks to Carol Miller, who took my notes and words, moved them around and organized them into stories, retaining my personality and my way of expressing them. And then there's her husband Mike, who kept us focused and organized and handled all the layout and computer details.

I wouldn't be where I am today without all the encouragement, help, insight, and friendship of so many who have touched my life. I thank you all.

Dick's Letter of Appointment to the "Best Job in the World"

STATE OF NEW YORK
CONSERVATION DEPARTMENT

ALBANY, NEW YORK 12226

OFFICE OF
General Administration

Mr. Richard J. Lang   October 23, 1969
2441 Bullis Road
Elma, New York

Dear Mr. Lang:

I am happy to advise you of your appointment to the position of Conservation Officer in the Bureau of Law Enforcement at Buffalo, New York, effective October 2, 1969 at an annual salary of $6118.

The Law provides that the probationary term of this appointment is not less than eight nor more than twenty-six weeks. If a probationer's services are not satisfactory, the appointment may be terminated after the expiration of eight weeks and on or before the expiration of twenty-six weeks.

Your probationary term will continue beyond the minimum of eight weeks under the above conditions and your appointment will become permanent if you are retained after completing twenty-six weeks. Successful completion of your probationary period will depend on your satisfactorily passing the Law Enforcement training course.

May I offer you my best wishes for your success and happiness in your work with the Department.

Sincerely,

F. C. Du Charme
Director of Personnel

14

Dick in the mid-1980s

Environmental Conservation Officer's Duties

Just what does an environmental conservation officer, or game warden, do? Why do they wear that special uniform, why do they have a special car, and why do they carry a gun? A lot of people first coming into contact with an environmental conservation officer have these and many more questions.

The environmental conservation officer (ECO) is a police officer, but a police officer protecting the *natural* world, as opposed to police officers protecting the *human* world. They are charged with the protection of the state's natural resources, responsible for enforcing all the state's conservation laws relating to fish, wildlife, and environmental quality. This includes apprehending and processing any illegal hunting, fishing, trapping, or the illegal taking of any endangered species, timber theft, or pollution of the environment. The Division of Law Enforcement is also the lead agency in the investigation of all hunting related incidents.

In recent years, they've also become responsible for enforcing the laws regulating the handling of chemical spills, the regulation of solid waste, industrial and hazardous waste disposal, enforcing the laws relative to the returnable bottle law, and inspecting the sale of restricted pesticides.

Dick with illegal phosphates, circa 1974

ECOs enforce the Navigation Law, the Penal Law, Vehicle and Traffic Law, and the Agriculture and Markets Law. The Department has specialized units such as the K-9 unit and the Bureau of Environmental Conservation Investigation unit to handle the enforcement of these laws.

That's a lot of laws to remember, and a lot of potential violators to track down. And remember, ECOs typically work on their own in remote areas without any backup. This explains the need for a sidearm. They must be available to follow-up a lead at any hour of the day or night, no matter what the weather. That's why it's necessary to have a car at their disposal at all times. It takes a special commitment to be an ECO and not everyone enjoys it or excels at it. But for those that do, the feelings of accomplishment and the stories they collect are worth more than words can describe.

The Conservation Officer's Uniform

On October 2, 1969, I was appointed a New York State Conservation Officer. I had to report to the Region 1, (now Region 9) Buffalo office. I was this skinny kid from Orchard Park, meeting men that I respected and was in awe of. When I got to the office, the Regional Conservation Officer, Everett Larkin, and Assistant Regional Conservation Officer, Robert Kauffman, were there to greet me. They introduced me to the two secretaries who would be helping me stay out of trouble with my reports. They had plenty of experience; each one had close to or over 30 years service and I was only 28 years old. Looking back, I seemed so young.

Reports. Boy were there reports! Daily, weekly, and of course, monthly. What you did, where you drove, how many miles... miles were a big deal then. You had to average about 75 miles a day. If you did a lot more one day you had to cut it back the next day. I found that real tough for a young conservation officer. I was either going to drive across my territory or walk it. I wanted to know every inch of the county. But first I had to get some equipment.

After two hours of listening to everyone, in the door walked my partner of the next fifteen years. He came over, shook my hand, and said,

"Hi. I'm Kimp Vosburg."

He stood 6'1", with steel blue eyes and hair gone completely gray. The one thing I remembered about our first meeting was his voice. It was very comfortable, for lack of a better word. It could either get your attention or it could put you at ease. Because I was on his side, it put me at ease. We would not be working together for another week as I was scheduled to go to Albany and pick up my uniform and equipment.

Later that day it was time for Chief Conservation Officer Larkin to transport me to his home and pick up my first state automobile. There it was, a black full-size 1969 Chevrolet. I did not sleep very well that night, being full of anticipation about the drive to Albany to be equipped with my new uniforms.

I arrived at the Conservation Department in Albany, walked into the first floor office, and met Assistant Director, Paul Benoit. Mr. Benoit was from the Adirondacks, and had the reputation of being an officer's man. We exchanged pleasantries and he sent me down the hall where I met the Quartermaster, Colin Bursey. He was in a Class A uniform and looked very impressive.

We left his office and went down to what I felt was the basement, where there were mounds of different sized uniforms. Colin started matching shirts and pants, in both summer and winter weight, a gun belt, and a .38 pistol with a six-inch barrel. It looked very long. At that time I knew nothing about pistols. I also got an oversized gray wool sweater. It must have weighed at least five pounds, but it was very warm. Next came the hats, two Stetsons, and a winter sealskin cap with fold down earflaps. A couple pair of field pants came next, very stiff field pants. Footwear included one pair of black dress shoes, hip boots, and 16" rubber packs. Lastly, the one thing that made me feel most like a Conservation Officer, the Badge, number 224. That gave me an authority that I would never take for granted.

It was two o'clock and time to depart Albany for the four-hour drive back to Buffalo. Quartermaster Bursey had loaded my back seat full of uniforms and equipment and, as we said our good-byes, my head was spinning. I returned from Albany as a new recruit with a carload of equipment and paperwork.

I had no experience with sidearms or uniforms; this was a new experience for me. Those were the days of on-the-job training; there was no basic training school. You learned from the senior officers in adjoining territories, and they all had their own ways of doing things from paper work to patrolling. That Saturday I was assigned to work with Conservation Officer Harold Keppner. I'll always remember his first question.

"Is your gun loaded?"

I said no. Harry gave me this real strange look and said,

"Let's go outside."

No one had shown me anything about the .38 pistol or how to fill out my biweekly reports or how to wear my uniform correctly. Harry was very gracious and showed me how to load and be safe with my sidearm, and how to correctly wear my uniform and fill out reports.

I remember in those first few months how uncomfortable I felt in different parts of the uniform. But, after about a year, that green uniform with the black stripe down the side of the pants became familiar to me and I always felt special wearing it. I was proud to put those pants on with that green shirt, and the patches that said Conservation Officer.

Our state patrol vehicle always went home with us. We started our patrol and answered complaints right from our homes; it was a necessity to have that patrol vehicle right there. Over a few years I was assigned two unmarked vehicles, which we thought were great for blending into the environment. Then, about 1975, Albany said we were going to be assigned marked vehicles. How are we ever going to catch anyone, we wondered? It didn't make sense. For the next 25 years I found myself looking for ways to hide our vehicles a little better. And, you know what, it worked. I still caught drug violators, deerjackers and plenty of fishing violators. Either we all became a little smarter or it was not as big a deal as we thought.

Time passed and over my thirty-four years of service I saw many changes. The wording on our patches went from Conservation Officer to Environmental Conservation Police. Our summer shirts went from long-sleeved tan to short-sleeved green. Our winter coats changed the most over the years, for the better, and our issued Rocky leather boots were the best ever. A big change was our issued firearm. It went from a .357 six-shot pistol to a .40 caliber semi-automatic pistol, a big improvement. Other pieces of equipment also improved over the years. Two-way radios were a big improvement. Our flashlight was a new charger type. But two things remained the same, our green pants with the black stripe and our Stetson hat. They helped create our image. I was always very proud to be in the uniform of a New York State Environmental Conservation Officer.

Mouth to Mouth

I could not believe it. I was patrolling my sector of Niagara County by myself, without a senior officer, after being on the job only about a month. I was still trying to get comfortable in my uniform and state car. It was an exciting time, performing the job of my dreams.

I had stopped at my home to see if there were any complaints when the phone rang. It was the Lockport Police Department with a complaint of a deer in the Erie Canal. The location was an area where there were very steep banks.

I arrived to find many bystanders waiting around to see what the new game warden was going to do. I got in the small police boat with a special deputy who had a license to use a tranquilizer gun. I had never met the gentleman before, and found him to be quite a bit older than me, with a take-charge attitude.

I could see the deer struggling in the canal. We were about ten feet from the deer when the deputy used the tranquilizer gun to dart the animal. With a manila rope in hand, I was able to put the rope around the deer's head, but the animal had not calmed down and continued to swim and started to choke from the rope tightening around its neck. *I have to do something*, I thought. *All these people are watching to see what this new kid knows.*

All of a sudden, the special deputy grabbed the deer by the neck, pulled its head to his lips and proceeded to give the deer mouth-to-snoot resuscitation. *Eeeww! I hope I don't have to do this on the job.* I couldn't believe what I had just seen. With that, the deer seemed to relax and we were able to get it to an area where the banks were not such a problem. The deer was released, he climbed out and was able to run another day.

All this time the public must have thought we were heroes for saving the deer. I just went away shaking my head. *What did I just see? A man giving mouth-to-mouth to a deer!* That was the first and only time I ever saw that happen in my thirty-four year career.

1991
Dick and Gretchen & Misty

The Game Warden's Wife

A conservation officer needs many things to succeed at his job, dedication, commitment, a love of the outdoors, physical health, mental agility and, perhaps just as important as anything else, a wife who understands the stresses of the job and supports his efforts. My wife is Gretchen, but she could be any other game warden's wife. Let me start at the beginning.

Even before I became a conservation officer she encouraged me to pursue my dream. Once I knew I had became a conservation officer the real work started. The first job she took on was the feeding of baby wildlife. We were young and it was an exciting time caring for fawn deer, baby raccoons, numerous songbirds and the occasional orphaned baby skunk. She even raised a great horned owl from a downy puffball into the mature predator it was meant to be. Under Gretchen's care, most of our orphans did very well and were able to return to the wild healthy and strong.

She also became well-versed in conservation law, not from studying the law books, but from overhearing my many conversations with people at the door or over the phone and applying what she learned. All our phone calls were put on a log next to the phone and she would answer most of them. If she did not know the answer she would refer the caller to a list of appropriate agencies she always had handy. But she would still insist that I give the person a call back. She would say,

"They don't want to hear it from some lady; they want to hear from the game warden."

Gretchen is a great cook and this also became a means of support for me. Many a conservation officer knew that if they started or ended the day at Dick Lang's home they were sure to get an outstanding meal. We always had many officers willing to work the salmon fishing or the waterfowl hunters due to the great hospitality that Gretchen provided. For most of my career I had a boat assigned to me and she not only provided a boxed lunch for me, she also included the officer assigned to work with me.

One of the highlights of my thirty-four year career was the opening day of the waterfowl season. We would have a detail checking the Iroquois Refuge and the Tonawanda Wildlife Management Area for waterfowl hunters and Gretchen played a huge part in making this a success. We had active and retired officers from two different regions participate and Gretchen not only provided a healthy breakfast for whoever showed up, she also set out a noon bash for all the hungry officers.

And, when I retired, Gretchen just kept going. She did the Duck Opener for five years after I retired and now, eight years post-retirement, she continues to set up lunch engagements with many of the retired officers and wives at a centrally located restaurant. She also organizes a picnic at our home in the summer for retired families. She shows no sign of letting go of her responsibilities to the department or of forgetting all the people I worked with through the years. I would not have been as successful at my career if I had not had Gretchen by my side. She wanted the bad guys caught as much as I did and she did her part to help me do it. She was the best Mrs. Game Warden. Thanks Gretchen.

Game Warden's Wives
Front: Marie Keppner, Judy Mills, Diane Rupp
Middle: Val Case, Dixie Sporer, Kathy Rackl,
Gretchen Lang
Rear: Georgiana Praczkajlo, Georgia Bosela,
Carol Robishaw, Joan McCargo, Debbie Lohr,
Melissa Kuska

Taking Care of Orphaned Wildlife

I don't believe it was written in the job description for a conservation officer, but it was understood that raising orphaned wild animals was part of the job. It was just something that happened. People would drop off baby raccoons, you would get a phone call about an abandoned fawn deer along a busy road, or an owl would have fallen out of the nest. Of course I enjoyed it; what an education for our two young sons. And what a job for my wife! I may have been the conservation officer, but she played a major part in the young lives of these babies.

Most abandoned wildlife did very well. I don't know if we were just lucky or if those youngsters were tougher than I thought. We raised young pheasants until they were big enough to release. We watched young Mallard ducks grow up before our very eyes.

We cared for squirrels, deer and owls. And, most all of them grew to be healthy animals that could be released back into the wild.

The first young animal my wife and I raised was a fox squirrel abandoned in the City of Niagara Falls. At the time, I had a female Brittany spaniel that thought she ruled our house. All of a sudden, this young squirrel came into the house and she wasn't too sure about it. She stuck her head into the box to see what this naked critter might be, smelled it, and decided whether or not she should accept it. I could almost hear her thinking, *What is he bringing home now?* We started feeding it cow's milk using an eyedropper, then graduated to a doll bottle. In time, the squirrel was able to take baby Pablum from a doll spoon. As it grew, we allowed it to spend more and more time outside and, in time, it just naturally went off on its own, which is what you hope will happen with orphaned animals.

Then along came baby raccoons, so small their eyes were still closed. But one of my helpers saved the day. That same Brittany spaniel had puppy problems and created milk but no puppies. I thought, *Let's see if she will accept them and nurse them along.* By gosh it happened! There was my Brittany nursing a raccoon. Her motherly instincts took over and she went from being the hunter to being the mother.

Then there was the time I brought home a fawn deer that I rescued from a longtime violator. This was a wonderful experience full of memories for our two boys, ages seven and eleven. Fawn deer are very delicate creatures and can be tricky to raise. They cannot tolerate cow's milk, which gives them scurvy. We had to get milk from the vet and feed it from a baby bottle. In time, it graduated to eating grass and spending more and more time outdoors. Like the fox squirrel and the raccoons, in time it just naturally roamed further and further afield and finally went off on its own. Another success.

In 1976 I received a call about a Great Horned Owl that had fallen from its nest on the Bishop Road, in the Town of Hartland. When I arrived at the home, the owl chick was being held in a cardboard box. It made me laugh to look at it. There sat this dusty brown puffball with big eyes and a beak that would not stop clicking. Hooter the owl was trying to show me just how tough he was by clicking his beak. At this time my wife was just recovering from pneumonia and I did not want to ask her to feed it. I need not have worried. The top came off the box, the two of them met and I need say no more. She raised that owl to maturity. By September the owl had his flight feathers and would fly back to a creek on our property to hunt muskrats. One day we heard all this squawking and carrying on outside and there was our owl, sitting on the gutter of the house, holding a dead muskrat in its talons. He was preening and showing off, clearly saying, "Look at me. See what a great hunter I've become!" And we were as proud as parents could be!

What a great outdoor education for our two sons and the neighborhood boys. But we also learned about death, that no matter how hard we tried, we could not always save all those baby rabbits or songbirds. Pheasants especially could be cruel to their nest-mates. If they noticed a feather that looked the least bit abnormal on one of their siblings, they would start pecking at it, keeping at it until they drew blood and weakened the baby. We learned that putting Vicks on the damaged feather discouraged the pecking, but still, we could not save all the babies. Sometimes we would feed them in the evening, say goodnight, go to bed, and find them gone in the morning.

During the 1980's the policy changed from the conservation officers raising wildlife to having civilians who were licensed by the Department of Environmental Conservation do the job. These rehabilitators were average citizens who contributed their time and finances for the good of these young wildlife. From that time on conservation officers and their families raised very few orphaned wildlife. I'm glad I worked during the era that allowed me and my family to raise the young.

Opening Day Traditions

My wife, Gretchen, and I always felt a special bond with our retired officers. I especially liked to hear the old game warden stories. Many of their stories revolved around the opening day of waterfowl season.

Opening day was always a very special day in the life of a conservation officer. There was nothing like that first day, especially if you were patrolling the Tonawanda Game Management Area, the Iroquois Refuge, or Oak Orchard. It was thrilling for me to have the Tonawanda Game Management Area in my patrol sector.

The first two waterfowl openers I happened to be working alone. Both times they started the same way. The season would open for legal shooting at one-half hour before sunrise, but that meant nothing. All of sudden I would hear a shot a half mile away. Looking at my watch, I saw it was 20 minutes before legal shooting time. With that one shot, approximately one thousand waterfowl hunters would start shooting. Being the young buck that I was, I would run with my hip boots, a shotgun, and my hunting coat. Sometimes I would catch a couple of the early shooters. I always wanted to get the guy that fired the first shot.

One year, just before the season opened, the officers had a meeting in the Buffalo office. I was a very frustrated twenty-nine year old. The meeting was going well when Regional Conservation Officer, Ev Larkin, asked if anyone needed any help with the upcoming seasons. There were twelve officers in that room and they were all looking at me. So, I told all those old salts of my frustration with hardly making any apprehensions. I needed help and I needed it now. With that, Jack Hassett from Erie County and Morris McCargo from Wyoming County said they would come up for some late shooting on Saturday. That was the start of my help.

By the October 2, 1971 opener, I was more experienced and was more organized. I had made calls to Environmental Conservation Officers Don Becker and Harry Keppner and they had agreed to meet at my home where my wife had coffee and donuts. It was a starlit night, clear, with no rain, thank goodness. I knew by 9: 00 AM that it was going to be a bluebird day. I had no hip boots issued to me, so Officer McCargo said he had a pair he could loan me. Sure enough, I was running through some flooded duck paddies when I got a cold sensation in my right foot. Water was coming through a hole in the boot not over the top. Oh boy, these boots are not mine. Oh well, no time to worry about a wet foot. Get on with catching the bad guys.

I had dropped the other two officers off in a different area of this 6000-acre marsh and told them I would pick them up at 9:30 AM and discuss our plan. After that first shot was fired, it was bedlam, with all those guns going off at the same time, guys shooting into the air and shot falling all around you. At 9:30 AM we all met at the bridge on Ditch Road, breaking off to check various hunters. By this time, the noise had gone from heavy gunfire to the sporadic shot. The morning had turned into a calm, sunny, forty-five degree day. The ducks had disappeared, gone. I drove around the area checking numerous wood ducks, Mallards, and teal. I had written two tickets for unplugged guns.

At 11:15 AM we headed back to the house where Gretchen had a pot of beef stew cooking that smelled so good, and plenty of coffee, cider, and soft drinks with numerous pastries. What a celebration we had. Among the guests were numerous retired officers, the U.S. Fish and Wildlife Agent and active officers from Regions 8 and 9. As soon as an officer got to the door he was hit with questions, "How many cases and what was the charge? Did you get the guy that started the early shooting? Did you fall in?"

What good times we had on opening day.

I would still want to be a conservation officer. It was the greatest job there was.

Charlie Robishaw, Retired ECO.

Fishing in Lake Ontario

For me, fishing in Lake Ontario started very slowly. It was a time when the commercial fishing had ended. The blue pike had disappeared and the walleye pike had reached numbers that would no longer support commercial fishing. Then, in the 1960's, the lamprey eel invaded Lake Ontario and destroyed what remained of our lake trout fishing. An invasive creature, the eel hid in the ballast water of the ocean freighters, attached itself to the lake trout and sucked the life out of the trout. I have to give the U.S. Fish and Wildlife Service a pat on the back for finding a selective chemical that killed only the lamprey larvae. By 1971 the eels were under control and it was time to start stocking brown trout again.

Dick in the mid-1970s

In March of 1971 my partner, Kimpton Vosburg, and I met the fish-stocking truck as it arrived in Olcott. This was the first stocking of trout in Lake Ontario in a long time and many fish biologists from the Olean Office had come to see the new fisheries in Lake Ontario. The trucks arrived from the fish hatchery in Caledonia, New York, and I watched as the driver maneuvered the big tank truck over to the east pier on Headley Boat Docks.

This was a first for me. I had never been involved in stocking fish in creeks, lakes, or ponds, but I knew I would enjoy it. The top of the tanker was unscrewed and the driver was handed a dip net. The net went in empty and came out full of wriggling brown trout, thousands of shiny brown trout.

No one knew if this experiment would be successful in reviving fishing in Lake Ontario, but we were hopeful. Then came the stocking of Coho salmon in Wilson Harbor, Chinook salmon, lake trout and the beautiful rainbow trout, all stocked from the lower Niagara River to the Salmon River close to Oswego, New York.

In order to monitor the fishing on the lakes, I needed a boat. My first state boat was a 25 foot "Winner." It was a winner all right, in more ways than one. It had seen its first tour of duty on the Kinzua Dam, in Cattaraugus County and now it was being delivered to Olcott, on the shores of 18-Mile Creek. I was very excited, my first patrol boat assigned just to me. I remember the first time I took it out. Easy does it as the boat slid into the Olcott Harbor. It was time to prime the engine, hit the starter and see what happened. I moved the gas lever forward ever so slowly. Hey, this seemed okay. Watch out fishermen, here comes the game warden. I was feeling pretty good, and I knew the next time I would take on Lake Ontario. The state had given me permission to rent dock space at McDonough's Marina. As I tied up "Winner" I told myself I would be back in the morning.

I had just finished my supper that evening when the telephone rang. It was the Niagara County Sheriff's Department asking me if I had a 21-foot fiberglass boat, green and white in color, docked in Olcott.

"Yes I do."

"Well I'm sorry to tell you Dick, but your boat sank."

"My boat sank? What happened?"

"Mr. McDonough called and said it had sunk, that's all I know."

"I'll be right there."

I drove quickly to the marina, parked the car, and descended the stairs to my dock. Looking over the dock I could see the outline of my green and white patrol boat. It didn't look like I would be checking any fishermen in Lake Ontario tomorrow. Mr.

McDonough said he would bring the boat to the surface the next morning. I arrived at 9:00 AM sharp to find my boat hanging in a sling above the water. I asked Jim,

"Have you seen any problems with it yet?"

"Sure do," he replied. "There is a two inch gash in the fiber glass that was never fixed."

So, back on the trailer it went and over to McDonough's Marina. From that day on the "Winner" was a problem.

Front row: Gene Tuohey, Jerry Sporer, Dick,
Back row: Chuck Robishaw, Harry Keppner,
Don Becker, 1969

Fall, an Exciting Time of Year

Conservation officers react to the changes in the seasons just like the migratory birds. In the fall, the changes seem especially noticeable as the leaves change colors and the days grow shorter. Most everyone reacts to these changes. Then there are the changes that only a conservation officer feels.

Some of my most favorite memories have occurred in the fall. I remember many beautiful, starlit, fall evenings sitting on the porch and hearing a dog bark way off in the distance. The bark is different than it's been all summer. It has a more hollow, haunting sound to it. Then there are the Canadian geese. The sight and sound of their flight is always exciting to me, I can never get enough of that sound. It's like they're saying, "We're leaving and, if you're smart, you'll follow us." But, of course, I never do. Then comes the day when I open the door, notice my state car covered with bird droppings and at the same time I hear the squeaky sound of a large flocks of blackbirds that have congregated on their flight to a warmer climate.

As I walk to the back of my 65 acres, I stop in my Christmas tree plantation and notice that the buck deer have become active. They've decided to use my soft-needle spruce trees to rub the velvet off their antlers. That gets me mad; go rub on a hardwood tree! I tell my son, who hunts deer during the archery season, "Go behind our house and kill a buck deer." Sometimes he does and other times he doesn't.

I look across my marshes and notice a scene that takes me back to my childhood, the sight of freshly built muskrat houses. For a period of time they continue to grow in size and then just stop. I enjoy looking into a marsh and seeing a muskrat house; it gives me the feeling that everything is okay. Then I frighten a group of five squeaking wood ducks. They are so quick and the male is so beautiful with all his multi-colored feathers.

Finally, I notice the sky...I love the changing of the clouds at this time of year, the huge, billowy, white clouds that always seem to be moving. I find myself taking in a deep breath of fall air and thinking to myself, "Thank God I have this job and thank God I am alive to enjoy it."

Late 1940s
Dick's father, John Lang, and Ray Ellis.

Working with the Federal Agent

Would you believe I did not know there were game wardens working for the Federal Government? When I started in 1969 as a New York State Conservation Officer, I was under the impression that the states had the power to appoint game wardens, but I was wrong.

The first Federal Agent I met was an individual by the name of Case Vendel, an agent working for the US Department of the Interior. I met him at a meeting called by Captain Larkin a week before the waterfowl season when Agent Vendel was to go over the latest federal waterfowl regulations. *Where was his uniform? Where was his gun? He can't be a real conservation officer.* Well, come to find out, these officers drive unmarked patrol vehicles and they do have guns, plus a lot of other interesting equipment.

On a hot July 14th, 1975, I was at my headquarters having a bite to eat when I heard the mail truck pull away. Opening the mailbox, I scanned the weekly sale paper for any curiosity items that people might have for sale. There, on the third page, I saw an ad: "For Sale, Eagle Feathers, Call Ken at xxx-xxxx." What I could not believe was that just ten minutes ago I had heard the Federal Agent, Len Lisenbee, talking to state officer, Walter Brownback, about setting up a meet. The best part was that they were only about thirty miles from me. I gave the guy a call at the number listed in the paper.

"Hi Ken," I said, "I'm calling about the ad you had in the Pennysaver about the eagle feathers."

"Oh yea, I have them."

"What kind of eagle?"

"I believe it's a Golden Eagle."

"Are they in good shape?"

"Oh yea, I have them in a display case."

"How much do you want for them?"

"Well, let's see. I'm asking $100 but will take $75."

"Okay, I'll be right over."

He gave me the address and, with that, I was out the door to my patrol car to call Len Lisenbee.

"923 to Federal Agent Lisenbee."

"This is Agent Lisenbee."

"Bee, can you give me a landline."

"Sure, in about ten."

I shut the vehicle off and went back inside. Moments later, the telephone rang. It was Len.

"Hi Dick, what do you have?"

"I just got off the phone with a guy by the name of Ken Layson, from Fredericksville, who claims he has a display case full of Golden Eagle feathers. We are not that far from there now."

"Can you give me the address?"

"Sure," I said, "Here it is."

Now, the hard part for me...waiting. In about an hour and twenty minutes, the unmarked car of Special Agent Lisenbee pulled into my driveway. Bee opened the door of his patrol car with a big smile on his face.

"Okay, what happened?" I asked.

"I offered him one hundred dollars and he said, 'It's yours'. Instead of taking the $100 out of my pocket I reached in and took out my badge and informed him that it was illegal to sell any parts of a Golden Eagle. He said he thought that if an Indian sold it to him it was okay."

Agent Lisenbee took the information he needed, informing Layson that the Federal Court in Buffalo would be notifying him as to the amount of the fine.

"Bee, where is the Eagle?"

He opened the trunk on the Dodge and there were the feathers of a Golden Eagle, all skinned out, starting at the neck and complete all the way down past the tail and under belly. It looked like a very nice display case.

1975
Conservation Offices with Mounted Golden Eagle

I was happy it had all worked out, with me reading the local paper and the Federal Agent close enough to take immediate action. What great timing. As my former partner used to say, "Stay out of the hot sun."

Equipment Changes

Our state vehicles became our second home. I always thought of my state car as my home on wheels. What changes occurred in my five decades as an environmental conservation officer!

My first state car was a black 1969 Chevrolet. The things I remember about the car were that it was unmarked, had no power steering and no AM radio. I guess the powers that be thought an AM radio might be a distraction. Or, maybe having a radio simply put the bid over the top. I personally liked the full-size sedans, but some officers liked the different varieties of jeeps or other SUVs.

Winter 1969 - First State Car

As of 1971, a new day dawned. We were now *police* officers, no longer *peace* officers, and with that new title came new responsibilities. The fun part was pulling up to a street light and watching the drivers in the vehicles next to you opening and closing their mouths while trying to read the words off the state shield on your door. No one had ever seen this vehicle before. Who are you? What do you do? It seemed to take years before people became comfortable with seeing a conservation officer's vehicle.

I believe it was 1974 when we started to get marked autos. They were American Motors automobiles with a single red light on the top. The first vehicles had "Conservation Officer" across the trunk and the state shield on the two front doors. Then, in the 1980's, they put "Environmental Conservation Police" on the trunk in big 4-inch letters. Well, we all thought, there goes our cases. We will never catch anyone with this marked car. But you know what? I could still put my state car in a place where no one could see it or park right in a big parking lot and I would still get cases. So I guess that story of marked automobiles not getting any violations was just not true.

Then came my first issued sidearm. It was a 6-inch colt with a three-inch belt that held handcuffs and a pouch for the issued .38s. It looked impressive because of its large size but a .38 caliber had a hard time finishing off an injured deer. We had no academy training; we simply trained with the senior officers in adjoining territories.

Then came the .357 magnum. It came in a four-inch frame with a two-inch belt. Now when I got in my patrol car it did not settle under my ribs. It felt comfortable, and I could breathe while I drove. After becoming proficient with the .357 magnum, the department came out with a new issue, a 9 mm Glock semi-automatic pistol. It held as many rounds in the clip and chamber as I used to carry in the belt loops for my .357.

Sidearms, rifles and shotguns...no matter what the weapon, I always felt our firearms training officers were the best. I could not have been trained by better officers. I never wanted to screw up. At the time of my retirement my belt was really full. I was carrying a .40 caliber Glock semi-automatic pistol, ammo, a baton, handcuffs, and pepper spray.

Public Relations

I always enjoyed meeting the public, even in a law enforcement role. The older officers seemed to enjoy the down and dirty aspects of the job, but to me there was always a lot more to it. I remember when I was in my teens and early twenties, how much I would hang on every word the conservation officer said. I attended meetings at the 4-H center and different sportsmen's clubs just to listen to them. So I was determined that, when I made the change to conservation officer, I would give back to the outdoor public my knowledge of what these men had given to me.

I felt that this became one of my strong points. Standing in front of a crowd of people can be hard, but the more I did it, the easier it got. I realized one thing was very important: know your subject matter.

And always be prepared. If I was not prepared, the sportsmen at the local club would know by the answers I gave. Whether I liked it or not, I was always on display, but from my early training I liked it.

I would always do my research and I usually had props to take long with me. When talking at the 6th grade field days in June I would always have large 16x20-inch pictures to show what a conservation officer did. I enjoyed taking pictures of the different activities and always had my camera in my state car. If I heard a call to a near-by officer, I would do my best to get a photo of the incident.

I also had a slide presentation explaining the different duties of conservation officers and showing various wildlife we came in contact with. That way I was prepared to go to civic groups or to sportsmen's clubs. I also had many different mounted wildlife specimens that I knew the young people would enjoy. Many of these mounts or skins I obtained from the Buffalo Museum of Science, with whom I had a great relationship. I would take them many different hawks, owls, ducks, fawn deer, and songbirds and, in turn, they would use their freeze dryer to make mounts for me for my youth education classes. We both benefited from the relationship.

Together, all these items provided me with a great collection of props to take to classes: large pictures of what a conservation officer did on the job, many different mounts and skins, a slide show and my last prop, myself in my green uniform with my gun and Stetson hat. For thirty-four years, this collection worked great and allowed me to present fun, informational presentations to more groups than I can remember. I always had a feeling of satisfaction when other officers within my region would ask to use my slides and pictures for their talks. I felt that public relations was just as important a part of the job as law enforcement.

I went to many outdoor shows representing the New York State Environmental Conservation Department. I was very proud to be assigned to these shows. During my career I went to Toronto, Cleveland, and Buffalo outdoor shows. I was also assigned to the Erie County Fair, and the Niagara County Fair. Then there were the conventions that were held in Niagara Falls or Buffalo. There I met people from other state agencies and representatives from the fishing or shooting sports.

I also made it known that I would like to participate in the Department of Environmental Conservation Displays at hunting and fishing shows in and out of state. I enjoyed meeting the public at these events. I was assigned to work the Cleveland, Ohio show twice, the Toronto, Ontario show once, the Buffalo show many times and the New York State Fair once, as well as many county fairs in the area. One side benefit was that I would frequently receive information that someone trusted me to develop into a case.

Whenever I had my uniform on I wanted to represent myself and the department in a positive way. I always made sure my uniform was clean, my shoes were shined, and I always had my state equipment ready for inspection. I felt I was always doing public relations, whether I was in a restaurant enjoying a meal or if I was in a duck marsh enforcing the waterfowl regulations. When stopped in a restaurant, I always wanted to provide the best information available to the public. Being in the field and having contact with hunters and fishermen afforded me the opportunity to build a positive relationship for the department and myself. I was always on display and felt I had to conduct myself in a way that reflected positively on all conservation officers. The whole department was being scrutinized by the way I conducted myself and I wanted to give my best impression. As a conservation officer, I felt it was an important skill to meet people and develop a relationship where I would be trusted.

I always made sure I was presenting the views of the Department of Environmental Conservation, not my own personal feelings. I always tried to be sure all the information I gave out was correct. If I did not know the answer, I would tell the person that I would get back to them. I did not run from the questions I did not know; having to look up the answers kept me sharp. I wanted to have the reputation of answering complaints, returning calls and getting people the information they requested.

During the last ten years of my career Albany started a program called EAGLES that was right up my alley. As part of this program, I would go into the different schools and give talks to elementary and junior high children on fish, wildlife, laws, and outdoor lore. It was something I really enjoyed. These students were the next generation of outdoor youth and I always wanted to set a good example on how I felt the outdoors should be treated.

In 1980 I received a phone call from Captain Fred Ott of the Buffalo Region telling me I had received the award as Conservation Officer of the Year. What a thrill to be given such an honor by my peers. When reading my biography it was mentioned that one of the reasons I won was because of the initiative I had taken in developing a slide presentation of a conservation officer's duties. I also developed a conservation law question and answer form that was published in the New York Conservation Federation monthly publication.

I felt public relations was a continuing process of working to gain the public's trust and confidence. It took time to become comfortable with and some officers never did. From my early years with the department until my retirement, I always enjoyed it.

Sixth Grade Field Days at Royalton Ravine Park
early 1970s.

The Deer in the Bathtub

It was November of 1969, my first year on the job, and I was working with my lieutenant checking duck and pheasant hunters. He was my senior officer for the day and, as we were driving through the county, he was informing me about all the written reports we were required to do. It was about 6:00 PM and we had one more complaint, to tag a car-killed deer that had been hit earlier in the day.

The day had turned into a rainy and very dark night, making the house difficult to find. As we pulled into the driveway, I did not notice any deer hanging from a tree. I thought that was a bit strange. Going to the door, I introduced myself, stating I had come to tag the deer and expecting the lady at the door to tell me it was hanging behind the house. So, I was surprised when she said to come in and follow her. She took me to the bathroom where I saw a most unusual sight.

The deer was all skinned and gutted and floating in the bathtub. With the hide off and legs removed it somewhat resembled a human being. There was a film of blood floating around the deer and, to me, it was quite an eerie sight. After issuing the tag, I got back in the state car where my lieutenant was waiting for me.

"How did it go?"

"You won't believe this one."

After relating the story to him, he just shook his head as we drove away.

Dick and Gretchen with his parents,
John and Grace Lang

The Channel 2 Visit

It was a Friday, just prior to opening day of pheasant season in the best pheasant-hunting county in New York State. I got a call from a WGR TV reporter asking if he and a cameraman could follow me around for the day. He said he wanted to see a hunting accident. A hunting accident?? In my county?? NOT!! They just don't happen, not up here in the flat lands.

***

Monday was opening day at my home. Family and friends had congregated at our house and the road was full of cars waiting for opening time. It was a beautiful morning. What a sunrise! The trees sparkled in reds and yellows, and the air had that crisp fall bite to it. All of sudden, like on command from some higher being, the hunters were in the fields, dogs were barking and it sounded like World War III. Pheasants were flying in all directions when suddenly I heard a voice a short distance away, just close enough that I could hear the hunter yell out,

"You shot me."

Oh my God! I thought. It really happened; someone got shot. *I hope his injury is not serious.* I started to run in the direction of the shooting with the reporter and cameraman following me. Moments later I found the victim in a grassy field holding his face. He took his hand away and there was a red spot in his puffy cheek. One pellet from the shooter's shotgun had hit him in the cheek. The shooter was quite upset and apologized over and over. The victim was in a hurry to get to his vehicle and to the hospital in Lockport to remove the pellet. While this was all going on, I took a statement and other pertinent information from the shooter. I informed the shooter and the victim that I would be calling on them in a couple of days. The reporter thought he had quite a story.

We were now alongside the road and the reporter wanted to do an interview with this rookie conservation officer. My first interview. Boy, was I nervous. The reporter put his mic right in my face, asking me many questions about what was going to happen next. After the interview he thanked me and went his way. I still could not believe this had really happened to me. The reporter wanted to see a hunting accident and it had really happened.

That night, we could not wait to see the six o'clock news. I felt they did a great job. I tried to get a copy of that video many times over the years, but they would not release it.

Oh well.

Front row: Kimpton Vosburg, Fred Ott
Second row: Morris McCargo, Jack Schlagenhauf

Boy Were We Lucky

My job had many perks, but one of the surprises I never imagined was "working" with all kinds of fun pieces of equipment. Those were the days. Civilians thought all these items were so cool, but to own them yourself was next to impossible. Thanks to my job, I had them all at my disposal any time I needed them. Yes, I had a boat, a snowmobile, and an ATV. I considered myself very lucky.

To start with, I had no previous training in any of these recreational sports. Boating was the first activity to which I was indoctrinated. The Regional Conservation Officer, Everett Larkin, said,

"Dick, you will be our second boat operator, right behind Officer Becker. When he is unavailable you will be the boat operator."

Sounded great to me.

It was a Tuesday morning and I was to meet Officers Becker and Keppner at Rich Marina, along the Niagara River in Buffalo. I arrived at 8:00 AM. In pulled the two Erie County Officers to teach me everything I needed to know, from cleaning a boat to its operation. I had heard stories that this boat was very powerful. As soon as I saw it I was very impressed. It was a 27-foot Chris Craft with twin Corvette engines. Officer Keppner yelled, "Get aboard!"

The boat was stored in a covered boathouse and every sparrow in Buffalo had been crapping all over it. Officer Keppner said,

"Dick, get out the boat brush and clean off the bird crap and the spiders."

No problem, I can do that. Officer Becker called into the Buffalo Office,

"Buffalo, we are under way on Lake Erie patrol."

As we left the boathouse, I could tell that this boat was built for speed. Both engines were rumbling in unison and Don Becker was steering the craft. As we pulled out into the river Don said,

"Here Dick, slide behind the wheel."

It was a big steering wheel, but there were only two gears, forward and reverse. That was easy. The speed was another issue. Slow is good but too fast can get you in trouble. Harry Keppner was explaining the gauges to me as we headed up river for Lake Erie: oil pressure, rpm's and water temperature.

"Dick, make sure she does not overheat and that you have good oil pressure."

Once we were into the lake Harry said,

"Open her up."

I pulled down on the throttle and my head jerked back. This thing is fast! The thing I disliked most was the noise. Those twin inboards were so loud I had to scream at the other officers so they could hear me. Now it was time to check some fishermen. I let off the power and the boat's forward motion slowed as we are approached a small boat. I had to be careful, since the boat didn't have any brakes, just a reverse. So, I moved it slowly into reverse and, oh boy, does that make a difference. Hey, this could be fun!

We introduced ourselves,

"Hi gentlemen, conservation officers checking your fishing licenses and fish please."

"Sure officers," they said and pulled up a stringer of smallmouth black bass. All legal, licenses good. Okay, let's go find some more fishermen.

Those Buffalo Hunters

It was a sunny, beautiful Tuesday, the second day of pheasant season, and I had the day off. I had made arrangements with one of my good buddies, Dick Osborne, to go pheasant hunting. I had a female Brittany spaniel and my buddy had one also. The dogs were in the car and we had picked out a spot about fifteen minutes from home. As we made a left onto Town Line Road, I noticed three hunters working a buckwheat field walking towards the road. I said to my buddy,

"Let's watch this."

Just like it was planned, a big rooster pheasant exploded out of the grass in front of the dog and started to fly across the road. Bang! The rooster fell onto the road. *This cannot be true; he just shot a pheasant over the highway. Now what?* Getting out of my car, I walked towards the three pheasant hunters, who were all congregated around the dead pheasant.

There was a middle-aged man, two teen-aged boys and a fast-moving, mixed-breed dog. I identified myself as a conservation officer and waited for their reaction. As we were discussing the violation, I saw a car pull out of a nearby driveway and head our way. It turned out to be the grandfather of the two boys. He jumped out of the car, leaving it parked in the road, and started yelling at me. He was screaming about all those no-good Buffalo hunters who come out and trespass and "shoot all our pheasants illegally." Since it was my day off, I informed the four men I would see them the next day. The older gentleman got back in his car and, still complaining about those Buffalo hunters, threw his car into reverse and ran over his own mail box.

The following day, dressed in full uniform and driving my state car, I returned and knocked on the door. I was welcomed into the living room by the elderly man's wife. Both the man and his son were very calm this time. I tried to explain that it was a violation of the conservation law to discharge a firearm across a highway. But all the time I was explaining this, I could not take my eyes off the elderly gentleman's feet. They were resting on a stool in front of his chair and I couldn't believe what I was looking at.

He didn't have any socks on, just a thin band of fabric around his ankles where his socks should have been. His socks were non-existent! The only thing left resembling a sock was the sock band going around his ankle!

I ticketed the son for discharging a firearm in such a way that the load passed over the highway. I left, shaking my head at what I had seen. Just another day in the life of a conservation officer!

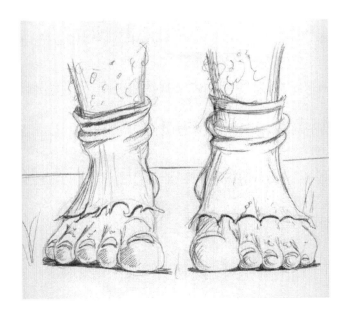

The Pheasant Hunter Who Crawled

The fall of 1971 was beautiful, with very little rain, and above normal temperatures. The lack of rain had created a very dry October. It was my second year as a conservation officer and I had been patrolling by myself for some time. I was being very aggressive, trying to be everywhere, check everybody, and catch as many violators as possible.

It was the first Saturday of pheasant season and there were hunters everywhere. It was one of the best pheasant seasons I had ever witnessed, but it seemed that the harder I looked, the worse it got. What I mean is that I could not find a violation for the entire first week and I was in the best pheasant county in New York State. Things were just not clicking. I looked at my watch. It was 11:45AM and, since I was near my home, I figured I might as well get some lunch. By now I must have some complaints waiting for me.

I made a right-hand turn onto my road looking at hunters, dogs, and vehicles on both sides of the road. I stopped and asked some questions,

"Did you see any birds? Can I check your hunting license?"

Coming in sight of my home, I saw a young hunter in his mid-twenties standing next to a small creek. He had not seen any birds and was quite disgusted.

"Officer, you must know where some birds are."

"This is as good as any place. Give it another try."

I wished him luck and drove another 200 yards to my driveway. Exiting my state car I had a good view of the large fields around my home. Walking into the house I called,

"Hi Honey, how many complaints do I have this morning?"

We always kept the complaints on a notepad next to the phone.

"None so far. Lunch is ready," she said, "Let's eat."

After eating, I got up from the table, and was placing my dishes in the sink when I heard a shotgun blast go off. It sounded like it came from that young hunter I spoke to just twenty minutes earlier. I went out the front door, and stood on the porch. Sure enough, there he was, standing in the road. While I watched him, a flock of blackbirds flew over the road and Boom! He shot right from the highway! He had seen me pull in this driveway and now he committed a crime right in front of me. Wow! I'd finally seen a violation.

Being in good shape, it only took me a moment to reach the car, but he had already disappeared. Pulling out of the driveway, I headed down the road to the bridge. Where did he go? His vehicle was still there. Only moments had gone by; where could he have gone? I bet he was hiding in the bushes. I quickly parked next to his car, and slowly started searching the area, walking slowly and stopping often to look and listen.

I still could not see him, but I could hear that dry goldenrod breaking. He was not fifty feet from me when I saw him crawling away from me. His shotgun was in one hand and his head was turned, looking over his shoulder, as if I did not see him. I yelled,

"Get up and come over here!"

When he stood up he had this sheepish look on his face, like he had just eaten one of those blackbirds he had shot. There in the road was his spent 12-gauge casing.

"I believe you knew that you could not shoot from the road, why did you?"

"Well, I hadn't had a shot all day and when those blackbirds flew over I just had to shoot."

I issued him the information to appear in Royalton Town Court on Tuesday night. He appeared as requested and I called him before the Justice who asked how he wanted to plead.

"Guilty."

"That will be fifty dollars."

As he pulled out the money to pay the fine, I looked into his wallet and saw lots of cash.

"Why do you have all that cash?"

"Well, I heard you guys were pretty tough, so I brought five hundred dollars."

"Well the fine is only fifty dollars this time. Don't do it again or it will be a lot more."

Another happy customer.

Roadblocks

When I think of roadblocks, I think of deer season. Roadblocks are a joint effort set up by the wildlife biologist and law enforcement as a means of checking the health and age of an animal, usually deer. They check its teeth as an indication of age, its antlers, and its general health. Then, there are the roadblocks used for a spontaneous check. These are set up by environmental conservation officers, either alone or with the help of a fellow officer, at a place where the road was not heavily traveled, but where you knew there was a good possibility of someone trying to sneak an untagged buck home by taking the back road.

There was always a roadblock set up the night of the first day of deer season. The lieutenant would have been in contact with the New York State Police and a time and location would have been set. The lieutenant then notified the officers under his command to meet at a pull off near the roadblock. Many times deer season opened with snow and cold winds, pulling the temperature down below freezing. The troopers had flares out on the highway and we would begin to look for deer hunters. The flares got the attention of approaching vehicles, alerting them to slow down and we would look into the vehicles with our flashlights. If we could see guns, hunting clothes or a dead deer, we would direct them over to an area where officers would check the deer license and tag to make sure some guy was not using his wife's big game tag or trying to take a doe on a buck license. We also made sure any firearms were not loaded.

One roadblock that stands out in my memory is my very first big game hunting season. I was directed to meet my lieutenant and three other conservation officers, along with three state troopers. The block had been in progress for about twenty minutes when the lieutenant ordered a hunter out of his vehicle and asked him to open his trunk. The man had just turned the key to the trunk when another vehicle appeared, moving much too fast for conditions. My first thought was, this guy is out of control. Officer Keppner was yelling, "Slow down, slow down!" But the guy just kept coming. The hunter who had just opened his trunk could not get out of the way fast enough. BANG! He was pinned up against his trunk. Everyone was screaming orders at the guy who was driving the car, "Put it in reverse, back it up, be careful." The hunter pinned against the trunk was trying to keep his composure, but you could tell he was in a lot of pain. The lieutenant called for an ambulance to transport the injured hunter to a hospital and I helped him over to the door and eased him in. It turned out his leg was broken.

I remember a spontaneous block on Route 77 and Lewiston Road. It was the second Saturday of the big game season and you never knew how many hunters you might find. But, for every hunter you checked out, you also checked out the family going to church or coming back from shopping. I remember many strange looks when I shined my flashlight in the window and asked it they had any guns in the car or if they had been deer hunting today. But, sometimes we hit the jackpot with our surprise checks and found untagged deer, a loaded gun or a license violation. That made it all worthwhile.

1987
Bob Kauffman, Les Wilson, Mike VanDurme, Neil Ross, Dick, Doug Case, Harry Keppner

Catching the Goldmans

It was October 29, 1979 and I had ten years on the job, a job I felt was made just for me.

On this day, I started my patrol at 9:00 AM, checking duck hunters along the eastern end of Niagara County. Violations were as hard to find as the waterfowl hunters. They just were not there to check. So, I went home to grab some lunch and see if there were any complaints for me. As I came into the house I greeted my wife with the usual, "Hi Honey. Any complaints?" Nothing today. So, I made myself some sandwiches and grabbed a glass of iced tea. I was into my second sandwich when the phone rang.

"Hello, Mr. Lang. You do not know me but I know you are the game warden and I do not believe in what the Goldmans are doing. If you go real quick you might be able to catch them with a deer in the trunk of their car."

"Where are they headed?" I asked.

"They are headed to their place on Dysinger Road."

"Okay, I know where that one is. What are they driving?"

"A green 1972 Plymouth."

"What direction are they coming?"

"They will be coming up Market Street and they left about five minutes ago."

"I'm on my way."

I made a quick mental list of things I might need...gun, tickets, coat, Stetson...okay, I was as ready as I could be and ran to the car.

It took me fifteen minutes to get to the location. Their name had been in my mental computer for a long time. I just might get a little lucky. We all have to have a little luck on our side once in awhile and maybe this was my chance. A quick glance at my watch showed seven more minutes have gone by. That's not bad. I looked down Market Street Hill for that big old '72 Plymouth, but nothing yet. I decided to take a quick look over by the Lockport Court House. Nothing. This was the route he was supposed to be taking. I checked traffic, made a quick turn and, *oh my God*, there he was, coming right at me. This could be the start of my luck. Quickly reversing my direction, I hit the switch on my overhead lights and with that, he pulled over right in front of the Lockport Police Station.

Approaching the vehicle I saw two men. I asked,

"Hi, guys. How has the hunting been?"

"Oh, we were not hunting," they replied.

"Well," I said, "if you were not hunting then you won't mind opening the trunk."

They were grumbling under their breath as I approached the trunk. As the trunk opened, what did I see but two small bore rifles and two shotguns.

"Gentlemen, it's time to show me your driver's and hunting licenses."

"But, we weren't hunting."

"Well," I said, "we'll discuss that later."

Looking over the trunk, I noticed deer hair everywhere. First I did a check of the firearms. The guns had a lot of wear on them, so who knew if they belonged to these two men. I was parked in front of the police station with two guys who have been on my mental list of violators. Taking pencil and paper, I wrote down the make of the firearms and the serial numbers.

"Guys, get back in your car. I'll be back in a minute."

Back at my car I called the Lockport Police. I explained who I was and that I had a vehicle pulled over in front of the station. I requested a records check on the four firearms and also requested an officer to assist me. They responded, "We'll be right out."

With the assistance of a Lockport Police Officer we again searched their vehicle and found only large amounts of deer hair. But, hair was all I needed to write a ticket for the illegal taking of a deer. This turned out to be a great case; a little extra work, but it all paid off.

1997
Dick, with Lawman of the Year Award

Picking Up the Bad Guy

To be a qualified police officer or, in my case, a
conservation police officer, you have to be physically
and mentally on your toes. I always wanted to project
an image of confidence that I could handle any crisis
I was presented with. I was six feet tall and weighed
160 pounds and I had quickness and agility on my
side. I believe that came from my wrestling
background. So, I had a good start, but the
confidence I had in later years did not come
immediately. It was a process; I had to grow into it.
Different situations and many arrests went into
developing that confidence.

One such incident happened in 1973. I had issued
tickets to four individuals from Buffalo for fishing
without licenses in the town of Lockport. I informed
them that if they did not take care of the charge I

would issue a warrant for their arrest and I would personally pick them up. It seemed a simple case.

Three of the four took care of their violations in a reasonable amount of time. The fourth did nothing. Four months went by. I kept checking with the court to see if he had taken care of the ticket. No, he had not been in. That got me mad. Maybe I was a little arrogant, probably because I had only been on the job for four years. But, I was not about to let him ignore me.

At this time, I drove a very large 1971 light green Dodge. It was unmarked, with no light bar or shields on the doors. It looked like a civilian's car except for a little antenna protruding from the roof. The defendant lived in what could be called a very undesirable part of the city of Buffalo. I had a good mental description of him: slim, about 5'6" tall, with short brown hair and he didn't seem to be dangerous to me. I found his street without much trouble and pulled up to his house. I could not believe my luck, he was sitting right there on the front porch. I had taken my uniform shirt off and opened the driver's door and yelled,

"Justin, can I talk to you a minute:"

Sure enough, he did not recognize me. He walked the thirty-five yards to my car and I said,

"Justin, get in the car. I want to talk to you a minute."

He got in the car without a question. I then told him he was under arrest for fishing without a license and I had a warrant for his arrest. I put handcuffs on him and we drove away. As we got closer to the judge's house, I called the State Police and asked if Judge Gallagher was available. They informed me he was and was awaiting my arrival. Now my defendant was starting to relax. We engaged in some conversation. All of a sudden it hit him. He asked me,

"What would you have done if I had run."

I said, "That's easy. I would have shot you."

"You would not."

"Well, you will never know, will you?"

Then he looked at his watch and asked,

"Can we get to the judge so he can sentence me?"

"Why the big concern?" I asked.

"So I can get supper at jail."

Well, we made it to Judge Gallagher's, who set the sentence at 15 days and, yes, I got him to jail in time for supper.

Mike Lucckino, Dick Lang, Kimpton Vosburg
National Hunting & Fishing Days, early 1970s

My First Chase

It was late one night in October 1971 when I was awakened by the Orleans County Sheriff's dispatcher.

"Dick, Conservation Officer Gene Tuohey is asking for your assistance with some deerjacking off the Meadville Road in the swamp. Can you be there?"

"Yes, I'll be there. Tell him I'll give him a call when I get in the area."

Checking my clock, it read 1:30 AM and I could hear it raining as I got into my uniform. I left the house and headed out into the night. Approaching Owens Road I called Gene and he gave me a quick update.

"Dick, there is a car spotting and they are looking hard for deer. They're coming your way."

With that bit of information I quickly looked for a spot to hide the car. The driveway to an abandoned farm was an ideal location and I backed the unmarked 1969 Chevy behind the lilac bush. Within moments I could see a faint light coming slowly in my direction. As the vehicle proceeded toward me I could see a light from the passenger side of the car scanning the fields. I could not believe the way my body was reacting. This was a new sensation, one I had never experienced before. My heart was pounding and my senses were on high alert. I was in full flight or fight mode and, as far as I was concerned, it was time to fight.

When the car came within one hundred yards of me I inched my way out to the edge of the road and turned on my grill lights and rear window lights. It was like an explosion. They tore out of there and I quickly figured out that they were not going to stop. We were both off on a high-speed chase. They headed west, then north, with me in hot pursuit. Somehow I managed to make radio contact with Officer Tuohey and gave him an update. We entered Orleans County and rocketed past two stop signs. Gene kept the Orleans, Genesee, and Erie County Sheriff's dispatchers notified as to my location. After many turns and speeds reaching as high as 92 miles an hour, we entered the Village of Akron, careened down a residential street and into a cornfield. Up ahead I could see the doors open and the interior lights come on as they came to a quick stop when their vehicle ended up on top of a dead elm tree. They tore out of the car and disappeared into the night. Before exiting my patrol car, I gave Officer Tuohey my location. Within fifteen minutes Gene, the Erie County Sheriff, and Conservation Officer Jack Schlagenhauf from Genesee County arrived on the scene.

The Vehicle was registered to a female, but that was no female doing the driving. With the assistance of the Erie County Sheriff we continued to check the area. While driving through the business section on one of our checks, Jack Schlagenhauf noticed three people walking away from us and one of them was a woman. This could be them. Jack told me to pull up next to them. I stopped the patrol car slightly ahead of them. Separating the three of them brought a quick confession from the 24-year-old female. She had let Tyler Stevens drive and his brother, Terry Stevens, would do the shooting. All three were issued tickets for having a firearm in the vehicle while spotlighting. The vehicle was towed to a secure location until the penalty was paid. I then met with New York State Trooper Britt, giving him a deposition for vehicle and traffic violations that had occurred during the chase.

In hindsight, I realized this was one of those nights you hear other officers talk about, the deer, the gun, the spotlight and the car ending in a chase. The funny part was, after I returned home at 9:30 AM I couldn't relax and go to sleep. I was so wired my eyes just would not close. I just sat in my rocking chair and rocked as fast as I could.

Dick, early 1980s

Deer Hunters with Artificial Lights

During the 1970's spotlighting really took off. There were two reasons for this: first, the deer population was exploding, and second, all the catalogs were selling those neat, new, hand-held lights. Those lights could spot a deer a long way off. This went on until the early 1990s. Since then it has not stopped completely, but it is much less frequent.

There is a feeling every hunter (and spotlighter) gets in the fall when the leaves start to turn color and the air gets that bite to it. As a conservation officer, I got that same feeling, whether it was a beautiful starlit night or if it was cold and raining. Only that illegal spotlighter and I knew that the time was now. It was also hard to explain, but my senses became very acute. My ears could hear a car approaching from long distances. In the dark, my eyes would pick up the sight of a light bouncing off a tree or rounding a bend in the road. As a civilian, I just did not have that keen sense of awareness, but as soon as I went "on the job" it was there.

You were not considered a true game warden until you apprehended a deerjacker. In our territory we all had our favorite spots to check for illegal jackers. Mine was the Tonawanda Wildlife Area. It was a mixed area of uplands, hardwoods, grass and, of course, marsh. It was a great place. Years ago someone, in their ultimate wisdom, had made this six thousand acre state management area with me in mind. I was in my comfort zone.

I remember one Halloween night with my boys safely home from their trick and treating when the phone rang at 9:30 PM. The voice on the other end said,

"Dick, there's a truck back in my field between Mann and Fisk Road . They're spotlighting but I haven't heard a shot yet."

"I'll be right over."

Sometimes I thought I was superman because I changed my clothes so many times a day and this was one of those days. Out of my civvies and back into my dress uniform. As I head out the door my wife asked,

"What's up?" She was used to these late-night disappearances!

"Complaint of jackers in the Wolcottsville area. Listen to the scanner if you want to."

I jumped into my state patrol car, making sure I had my flashlight, pens, and ticket book. Within ten minutes I was at the area in question, moving slowly and scanning carefully. Sometimes the god of the game wardens was on my side. By that I mean that I found a good position to park my vehicle so I could watch the spotlighters come slowly out of the field onto the road. I saw them coming. When they hit the road I hit my overhead police lights and, with that, it was like someone poked them with a hot poker and we were off. The race was on!

We turned right, picking up speed, but that ended quickly because they made a U-turn on a small, paved country road. Then we headed south for a short distance before leaving the road for a grass lane. The lane turned out to be shortcut to the next road. By now I was mad. My adrenaline was busting out of my pores, and I was going to catch them. As we hit the pavement, I knew what they were thinking. *When are we going to lose this guy*? I could see what I believed to be two males in the truck.

The next thing I knew, we left the road and raced across a front yard between a small ranch house and two big maple trees. Then it was back on the road for 200 yards before hitting a farmer's lane heading east. I can't believe this! I was still within 50 yards of them and still determined to catch them. Making a right turn onto the paved road we were now headed south at about 50 miles per hour. I spotted the power lines and wondered if they would make a left into them. Sure enough, that's what they did. But, like I said, the poaching gods were on my side, not theirs. Wham! I saw the truck jump up into the air and crash back down in a bunch of dogwood trees.

Jumping out of my green state vehicle, I approached the truck with my light in hand, prepared to draw my sidearm. I screamed commands at the two men:

"Exit the vehicle slowly with your hands where I can see them."

As one got out of the car he said,

"Hi Dick" and I realized I knew him!

What a chase! I was glad to be alive, but I was still mad. As I was chasing them, I had somehow managed to contact the State Police and tell them where I was. Sure enough, within a matter of moments two trooper cars and the father of the driver showed up. The father asked to speak to me.

"Sure, what's up?"

"Give them a break, they're just kids."

Give them a break?!?!?! Was I hearing him right?!?!?!

I raised my voice and squinted my eyes at him, speaking with barely controlled anger,

"They could have killed me, or doesn't that matter?"

I seized the gun, writing down the make, model and serial numbers. Then I wrote a ticket for the artificial light and possession of a firearm. Then I turned the vehicle and traffic violations over to the state police for prosecution.

Things had calmed down a bit by then and everyone was getting ready to leave. I got back in my vehicle to leave, turned the key and, guess what? It wouldn't start! *Where are the game warden gods now?* After numerous tries I contacted the State Police by radio and asked them if they would please place a phone call to a tow truck operator to come get me out of this remote area. Everyone had gone and I was in the front seat of my patrol car, head back on the headrest, realizing how lucky I had been during the chase. What good fortune that the car died at the end of the chase, not in the middle of it. Just one more exciting evening in the life of a conservation officer!

Fawn Caper

It was May 30, 1976 and we were celebrating Memorial Day with some good friends. The phone rang with an unusual complaint. The caller on the other end was an irate wife who had had a verbal argument with her husband. The caller yelled,

"Come up here right now and get this fawn deer that my husband has as a pet."

My guest, Hank Haas, was a New York State Trooper and he came along and listened to the story. Fifteen minutes later we were at her home. There in the hallway was a spindly-legged fawn deer. How did he get this fawn? She said her husband had seen this doe and fawn in the field behind their house. He had always wanted a deer for a pet and felt this was a good chance to get one.

"So what happened to the doe?"

"It's lying back in the woods behind the barn; he shot it."

I asked myself, now what kind of person would do this? We took the fawn, gave her the receipt and drove away.

For two days I could not get back and look for that doe. It was gnawing at me; I had to find that deer. Finally I got the chance. I had an idea where the animal would be. I parked my patrol car a half-mile away, divided the woods into sections and started scouring each section as thoroughly as I could. It was hot and there were lots of bugs. *Okay, here is the area, I can see the house, let's find that deer.* I kept taking sections of the woods and covering them very slowly. The bugs kept biting and I kept walking. After an hour of looking, I started asking myself questions. *Is this the spot or was she guessing?* Closing in on two hours of searching I was just about to give up when I spotted the carcass of the doe deer. I took pictures, found the bullet hole, took notes, and left the scene.

Now I was all fired up. Going to my local town judge, I got an arrest warrant for two charges, possessing a fawn deer without a permit and taking a doe deer during the closed season. It was one of my most unusual wildlife cases. The defendant was the type who had always wanted to be a wildlife buddy. Everyone else was always wrong, but not him. This is the type of person your gut tells you to be wary of. If he is trying to distract you and point the finger at someone else, look closely because he has a hidden agenda. But the defendant did not get away this time. He appeared before the judge and had to pay a fine.

Families

I became familiar with many families in my area, and I don't mean the ones I met in church on Sunday. These were the families whose names appeared in the local paper and on the police report...many times. It was sort of a family tradition with them...Grandpa did it, Dad did it, now we're doing it. These were the hard-nosed game violators, the game poachers, the criminals, and they really kept me on my toes.

One family was the Poller/Turner family. They had moved to the town of Hartland from Pennsylvania. There were two teen-age boys, Leroy and Fenster, and step-dad Mason Poller. Then there was the leader of the gang, Raylene Turner, a real "Ma Barker." This family would steal anything from guns to snowmobiles. I got the word from the New York State Troopers that this family could be very dangerous. They lived by their own set of rules, thinking the laws didn't apply to them.

In 1974 I read in the local newspaper that there were numerous house break-ins all within a short distance of the Poller/Turner home and I was confident they were involved. They had a passion for guns, dogs, and hunting. The price of raccoon pelts was starting to reach $25 and that brought out the bad guys who loved to hunt all night and sleep all day. I had seen Mason in the corner store on Route 104 and told him I had heard that he wanted a fawn deer just like the pet he had in Pennsylvania.

"Mason, this is not Pennsylvania and you cannot possess a fawn deer. If I find out you have one, you will be arrested."

"Don't you mind Lang, you won't find me breaking the law."

I knew it was only a matter of time until I found him with a deer. Call it a game cop's hunch. In May 1975, I received a call from a neighbor.

"Dick, Mason has a deer, a fawn deer."

"Where is it?"

"I saw him walking it around on a leash. It's in the stable next to the door."

At 1:30 PM I drove to the Poller home and knocked on the door, but no one answered. On a hunch, I looked in the barn. Sure enough, there was the little fawn chained to the wall. Glancing around, I also discovered three rabbit cages containing...not rabbits, but raccoons. I had told him,

"No deer, no raccoons."

The school bus stopped and Leroy jumped off, asking me what I wanted. I told him,

"Mom or Dad. Can you get hold of them?"

"Dad is on his way home."

A few minutes later, a dark truck pulled in the drive and Mason stepped out.

"Mason, I told you no deer and no raccoons. You did it anyway."

"We found the deer; it needed help. The doe had abandoned it."

"No, Mason, you picked it up."

Then two more cars pulled into the driveway. One was my partner Gene Tuohey, whom I had called earlier, and the other was none other than Raylene Turner.

This woman would give you the creeps. She was about 38 years old, solidly built, with jet-black hair. But what I will never forget were her dark black eyes. Piercing, they stared right through you. They looked like the devil was behind them. Simply put, she looked evil. She had complete control over the men and at once you knew she was the undisputed leader of the family.

I introduced myself and Conservation Officer Tuohey.

"I know who you are," was her only reply.

I felt very uncomfortable. I knew these people loved guns and I kept glancing at the upstairs windows, expecting a gun barrel to be pointed in my direction. I went to my patrol car and called the Wrights Corners State Police, and asked them to send a backup to the Turner residence on Black Creek Road. Then I turned my attention back to Mason.

"Mason, you are in violation of possessing a deer and three raccoons, and I will have to seize them."

"Oh no you don't," yelled Raylene. "Mason, if Lang takes that deer you go too."

"Please, Raylene, there is nothing I can do. He's going to take the deer and the raccoons."

Officer Tuohey helped me cage the raccoons and we put them in his car. The fawn we secured in my state car. Time seemed to stop as Raylene shot us her parting words,

"Tuohey, I like you, but Lang, I hate you."

With those "comforting" words ringing in our ears, we left. Gretchen and I raised the fawn and it did fine.

But, that wasn't the last we heard of Raylene Turner. She did kick Mason out of the house when the fawn left, just like she said she would. At our family Christmas celebration I heard on the news that Mason Poller had been shot. He had been delivering gifts to the boys when Raylene's new boyfriend shot him through the picture window of the house. He was hit in the chest and spent three days in the hospital before signing himself out.

Dick with the baby fawn, early 1970s

The Endangered Fur Coats

It was January 15, 1973, a short time after the new Endangered Species Law went into effect. It was a blustery Sunday and I was home reading the "For Sale" section of the paper. All of a sudden an ad jumped out at me: "Leopard fur coats for sale." That caught my attention. I got out the new federal and state laws pertaining to endangered species to make sure leopards were listed as endangered and they were. The store in question was one of the oldest furriers in the city of Buffalo and I thought it a little odd that they had not kept up with the new regulations. I checked the address in the ad against the address in the telephone book and everything checked out. I called Conservation Officer Don Becker, since the location of the store was in Don's area.

"Don, I was reading the Buffalo paper and found an ad for leopard skin coats for sale. How about we get together and check these coats out? Why don't we meet next Saturday, I will be in uniform and you can be in plain clothes."

"Sounds good, Dick. I'll meet you at the Buffalo DEC Office at 10:00 on Saturday. See you then."

Meeting at the Buffalo Office, we brushed up on the new Endangered Species Law and put the finishing touches on our first Endangered Species case. We decided to take my car since it was an unmarked state patrol car. I located a parking space where I had a good view of the store. Officer Becker would take the ad in, asking to see the leopard coats that were advertised for sale.

Twenty minutes went by before Officer Becker came out and gave me a wave to come in. We showed our identification and informed the owner that he was in violation of the Federal and State Endangered Species Law. There were three full-length coats that were shown to Officer Becker as leopard coats. We could not be sure what kind of coats these were; all we knew was that they had a lot of spots. We issued the owner an appearance ticket for Buffalo City Court and gave him a receipt for the three coats.

Next we discussed the case with Captain Frederick Ott, who was in charge of the Buffalo Office. The Captain made the decision to take the coats to Albany to have our wildlife pathologist, Dr. Ward Stone, look at them. Leaving early the next morning we arrived at Dr. Stone's office four hours later. After raising his eyebrows and making some funny noises, he came to the conclusion that the coats were not made of leopard skins. He pulled out one of those big scientific animal books of the cat family and I got a real education. I never knew there were so many wild cats with spots on them. The doctor then came to the conclusion that these coats were ocelot. This cat is found in South America and also has spots. But the big question remained, was it listed in the Endangered Species Law? Quickly going to the law we were relieved to see that the ocelot was also endangered.

The case was brought before the Buffalo City Court where I presented the charges that now read "ocelot" in place of "leopard." After much deliberation, the furrier was found guilty and lost possession of the ocelot coats.

Officer Don Becker with ocelot coats, 1973

The Wildlife Auction

It was Tuesday, March 14th, at 11:00 AM when the car radio came on.

"Buffalo to 152." (152 was my official car number).

"152 to Buffalo," I answered. It was Lieutenant Bob Kauffman.

"Dick, would you please call the office."

"It will be about fifteen minutes."

"Buffalo received."

Stopping by the Newfane Town Hall I used the town clerk's telephone to give the office a call.

"Hi Dick. Could you meet Officer Becker and the Federal Agent Lisenbee tomorrow?"

121

"Sure Lieutenant. What is this about?"

"Sullivan Auctions is having a mounted wildlife auction tomorrow at his building on Delaware Ave."

"Oh yes, I know where it is."

"Call Don and make arrangements. And Dick, wear civilian clothes."

Don and I met at the federal agent's office in downtown Buffalo. We were briefed by Agent Lisenbee who told us they expected protected birds such as hawks, owls, geese and ducks to be offered for sale.

"Where did all this wildlife come from?" I asked.

"From one guy, Fred Pierson, who is now serving a life sentence in prison for killing two missionaries in Texas."

I did not know much about this guy, but the stories I'd heard were pretty bad.

As we parked the car and headed up to the second floor of the auction house, we all started looking through the crowd to see if we recognized anyone. I didn't see anyone I knew and hoped the other guys didn't either. At 10:00 AM the auctioneer gave instructions and away we went. He started with one of the many deer heads. He sounded good, but I wondered how long this would go on. A deer head sold, then a wild turkey and a Mallard duck.

Finally, I saw agent Lisenbee nod his head. With that, he announced that the auction was over and we would be seizing all the federally protected wildlife. I heard some grumbling at first, but it ended quickly. I found it hard to believe that one guy could shoot so many state and federally protected species. There were hawks, owls, ducks, geese, and songbirds. My partner, State Officer Don Becker, said,

"You won't believe what I just loaded into the truck!"

"What's that, Don?"

"The mounted head of a buffalo."

"What's the story on that?"

"He and another guy shot it at night off the LBJ ranch in Texas."

Once the evidence was accounted for, that buffalo head found a home over the counter of our law-enforcement office. It was quite a conversation piece and always looked like it had a smile on its face.

At the sale, I saw a local character who was known to be pretty tight with a dollar. He bought two beautiful deer heads. I said,

"Hey, Merlin, where are you going to show off those heads?"

"Oh, I'll think of some place, but don't tell my wife."

"Why not?"

"Because she would shoot me."

That was the only wildlife auction I ever attended as an environmental conservation officer.

The Dead Grandfather

It was Thanksgiving Day, 1975, and I was busy checking deer hunters in all the hot spots throughout Niagara County. Only on the job for six years, I was determined to check as many hunters as possible. It was not cold enough to snow but it was raining; that meant that the hunters would be headed back to their vehicles sooner than if there was snow on the ground.

I had checked a lot of deer and listened to a few stories, but violations were few. As I headed west on Ellicott Road, going by the Dobson Farm, I looked at the house and buildings and saw a deer hanging in the barn. Hey, this could be a good check. As I pulled in the driveway, one of the sons, whom I knew as Tom, came quickly out of the house to greet me.

"Hi Tom. I would like to check that deer."

Conservation officers in New York are issued what we call Deer Report Cards. They are used by biologists to make a calculated deer take. Plus, it is a good way for an officer to get a check of the hunter's deer tag. Walking to the deer I asked Tom,

"Did you shot the deer?"

"No, no my Grandfather did."

"Who is he?"

"Henry Dobson."

I had never heard of him. I read the name on the tag and, sure enough, it read Henry Dobson. I knew of Joseph, Joseph Jr. (Joey) and Tom, but not Henry. The tag showed the deer was killed on today's date.

"Tom, let's get in my car where we can talk."

By then it was 2:45 PM and raining hard and I had to meet my family and go south of Buffalo for turkey dinner at Grandma and Grandpa Lang's.

"Okay Tom, tell me more about your Grandfather? Where does he live, phone number, where is he now."

This family had been on my radar screen for some time. The longer we talked, the more I felt there was some hanky-panky going on. After an hour he still had not told me where his grandfather lived.

"Who shot the deer, Tom? Was it you? Who?"

I knew a part of him wanted to tell me but he did not want to let the family down. One minute I was screaming at him,

"WHO SHOT THE DEER? WHO IS THIS DOBSON?"

Then, after a few moments of silence, I would be soft spoken and would say,

"Everything is going to be okay. Who is it?"

With that he started crying and said his grandfather has been dead for the past 19 years and that his father, Joseph, had shot the deer.

"How did he get this license?"

"He would go to the Hartland Town Clerk and represent himself as Henry Dobson and then go to the Newfane Town Clerk and buy a license in his name."

I glanced at my watch. Oh boy, it was getting late. My wife was going to be disappointed; it looked like we would be late for dinner. I had to finish this one right now. I went to my briefcase and took out a voluntary statement form.

"Tom, fill this out in your own words."

This was the kind of case a conservation officer dreamed of. A charge of taking an illegal deer, and making a false statement seemed to be adequate. He handed the statement back to me.

"Is this a true statement?" He nodded yes.

"Okay Tom, let's put the deer on the top of my trunk."

He loosened the rope and down it came, a nice 6-point buck.

"Tom, where is your father?"

"He and Mom went to Lockport to visit an aunt."

"Tell Dad I will see him tomorrow."

As I drove away I thought, what a great pinch. This is the type of violation that makes you feel good. I was proud of my interviewing. It had taken a while, but it was worth it. I was glad to put a dent into a game hog. These types are killers, not sportsmen. They just want to kill, not be a hunter who enjoyed the outdoors and obeyed the laws.

The next day at 2:00 PM I drove to the Dobson home. Joseph answered the door.

"Hi Joe, we have some business to take care of."

He was very quiet as he got in the passenger side of the car. Joe gave me his hunting license and the license in his dead father's name. I took the information off his license, issued two tickets, and gave him a receipt for his illegal license. He made some statement that he may fight the charges. I did not know on what grounds. I felt confident that my charges were good and there was no Henry Dobson.

We set the court time for 1:00 PM in Justice Wilburt Rathke's office. At 12:45 PM I presented the paper work to Justice Rathke, explaining the penalty section and what can happen to the license. The door opened to his office and Joe walked in. He had come right from the barn, wearing a dungaree jacket, pants with holes in them and dirt hanging off his leather boots,

"Sit down Joe, let's go over these charges."

Reading the charges the judge asked,

"Do you understand what I just read?"

"Yes."

"How do you plead?"

"Guilty."

"That will be a $1,000 fine for the illegal deer and $250 for the charge of making a false statement. Are you prepared to pay at this time?"

Joe reached into his overhauls and removed twenty $50 and $100 bills, a total of $1,250. The charge also carried a revocation due to the illegal taking of a deer. Joe lost his hunting privileges for five years due to his greed.

Word spread quickly about a violation as severe as this one.

Mark Mazurkiewicz, Dick, Wally Cain
in Buffalo Office Radio Room
2003

The Stolen Deer

It was early on October 9, 1975, when the moon was full and almost anything can and will happen. Just ask any police officer. There is more crime committed during that phase of the moon than at any other time. By 7:30 AM my phone was ringing.

"Hey Dick, this is Ralph Haskell down here in Gasport. I need your help; someone stole my deer."

"How did that happen?"

"Had it hanging in the back yard and someone stole it."

"Ralph, give me a few minutes and I'll be right there."

Ralph was not only a hunter, he was also the supervisor of the Town of Royalton. And he was hot, real hot. He told me he wanted that deer back. The deer wasn't a real big buck and didn't have a big rack, but if I was lucky I still might be able to identify it. It had a small, 6-point rack and the right rack was broken.

"Ralph, any of your neighbors hunt?"

"Yea, there is this kid who lives on West Avenue who hunts but I don't know if he is old enough. They call him Charlie, that's all I know."

"Okay, I'll see what I can do."

I called on the butcher shop in town and inquired if they had cut up a deer for a young lad by the name of Charlie. He opened up his pad and found the entry.

"Yes I did. I have a Charlie Peters who got one. He picked the deer up yesterday."

"What kind of rack did it have?"

"Kind of a scruffy 6-point. One side of the rack was broken."

Taking all the pertinent information, I was now ready to call on Charlie. It was 7:10 PM and I figured he would be home. I knocked on his door, the door opened, and there stood a husky teenager. As I introduced myself, I could see he was looking me up one side and down the other.

"Charlie, I understand you got a deer."

"Yea, I got one."

"Well I got these report cards and I have to fill one out on your deer. Would you please bring the tag to me?"

"Sure."

A few moments later he appeared with the tag attached to the antlers, the antlers I had been looking for. I know he did not shoot this buck; he stole it from his neighbor's back yard and claimed it was his. I also had the written portion of his big game license in my hand.

"Charlie, put your shoes on and come outside. I have a few questions to ask you."

As he exited the small home he shared with his mother I told him,

"Okay, there's the hard way or the easy way. How old are you?"

"Eighteen."

"Tell me the truth."

Well, he might have been a bad kid, but not that bad, not yet.

"I'm sixteen."

"Okay, that's better. Let's go talk to your mother."

"Mrs. Peters, your son did not shoot this deer. He took it out of the tree in Mr. Haskell's back yard. And he is not even supposed to be deer hunting yet. The license has the wrong date of birth by two years."

"Charlie, this is what I want you to do. Go to your freezer and put all the deer meat in a box with the antlers."

After issuing two tickets and picking up a box of deer meat, I left the Peters home and drove to the supervisor's home.

"Ralph, here is your deer. It looks a little different than the last time you saw it but it is all cut and wrapped."

He just shook his head and thanked me for retrieving his deer.

Dick, late 1970s

Interesting People I Have Met

During my thirty-four-year career working with the public, I met dozens of interesting people. Some were "interesting" in a good way; some were "interesting" in a not-so-good way. But, a few in particular were worth remembering.

The first interesting person I remember happens to be a female. You notice I did not say "lady," because after what I saw and heard, I did not think she qualified to be called a "lady." I always knew the day would come when I would meet the female of my dreams. Boy, was I kidding!

It was 11:00AM and I had just finished some paperwork that had to be mailed to the Regional Office when the telephone rang. The voice on the other end said,

"Lang, I want you down here NOW. I want to talk to you."

"Can you tell me what this is about?"

"It's my neighbor. He's shooting all the time."

With that, she hung up the phone. I drove down to a group of farms located in the lower east side of Niagara County. This area is inhabited mainly by hard working, law-abiding citizens. I looked up from my clipboard just in time to recognize the house number. As I exited the patrol car, I positioned my Stetson firmly on my head and walked up to knock on the front door. Suddenly the door swung open and a voice rang out,

"LANG."

"Yeesss" I replied in a sheepish voice. I had never seen this person before in my life, and she made it sound like we were the best of friends. She was a woman in her fifties, wearing dungarees, and a flannel shirt.

"Come on in here. Those damn neighbors are going to shoot my @#$% cows and then there'll be trouble."

She continued to go on with those heavy-duty swear words explaining in so many words what she was going to do to this family if they did not stop that @#$% shooting. I guess I always knew the day would come when I would meet a woman who could swear a blue streak.

Then, the rest of the family came in from the kitchen, her husband and a young man in his early twenty's. I stared at the boy, only this was no mere boy. He was huge, not tall, but thick. He looked to be about five-feet-ten inches tall and around 300 pounds, with a round face, no neck and deep set eyes. I figured I would need a train to stop him. As we shook hands, Jake was sizing me up like I was his next meal. At six feet, one hundred sixty pounds, maybe I could outrun him.

We left the house and Jake and Mrs. Humphreys gave me a tour of their farm. As we were dodging cow and pig manure, I found out that Jake enjoyed deer hunting. He not only enjoyed deer hunting, his favorite food was deer meat. As I prepared to leave, it was agreed that they would call me if they felt the neighbor was shooting recklessly.

Over the years, Jake and I developed what I could almost call a friendship.

Two or three times a year I would answer the telephone and it would be Jake. He would not start the conversation off with a hello, but with simply,

"Laaaang, you got any car-killed deer?"

"No, Jake, none at this time. But I will keep you in mind if I get one."

"Thanks." Click.

One deer season I was assisted by my good friend, wildlife officer with the U.S. Fish and Wildlife Service, Dan Smoot. Dan was a former state officer from Maryland who was now assigned to the Buffalo area. When he wasn't working on a duck season violation, he was helping me with late shooters, deer checks or salmon fishing violations. We had a lot of laughs together.

It was about ten minutes after one on a beautiful Saturday. I suggested we see if we could find some action on the Ditch Road. Dan nodded and started to scan the edges of the woods where they met the fields, looking for a red or orange hunting coat. Suddenly, one hundred yards in front of me, a big guy in a red hunting coat and cap crossed the ditch and stood on the side of the road.

"Dan, up ahead is the hunter I told you about."

He was on the passenger side as I stopped the patrol car. Bending over, he looked right past Dan to me and gave me his typical,

"Laaang, got any deer you don't want?"

"No Jake, none yet, but I'm looking."

As I drove away, I said to Dan, "I get the feeling I could be lunch."

Dan laughed and said, "I think you *are* lunch."

***

Not everyone I met was an outdoorsman, but I still consider the time I spent with some of them to be memorable.

Another interesting person I remember was Otto Klippenger. Otto lived in the town of Royalton and was in his early eighties when I was in my mid-thirties. He spoke with a German accent and stood about 5'10" with very broad shoulders. He first called me with a complaint of pheasant hunters trespassing on his property. It was one of those complaints that had very little information, so I drove out to get some more details.

"Mr. Klippenger, did you confront them?"

"Oh no, they had guns."

"Did you write down their license plate number?"

"No, I was afraid to leave my house. There were three men and they walked right past my posted signs. They never asked permission."

He was able to give me the type, color and year of the vehicle and the fact that there were three hunters. He seemed to be an interesting man. I left him that day only to return later to inform him that I had not seen the vehicle in the area.

As more time passed, he started to tell me about his early childhood. He had been raised in Munich, Germany. When WW I started, he was drafted into the German Army and sent to France to fight the Americans. To this day, he kept his dislike of guns. So, an experienced German fighter, capable of fighting our American soldiers and surviving the war, was afraid to confront three trespassers on his own property?! Well, the world is full of interesting people!

It was the greatest job. I would do it again any day of the week. I wouldn't just walk, I would run.

Frank Lohr, Retired ECO.

Trapping Muskrats

Whoever would have thought you could make a living off trapping beaver or muskrat in Niagara County? This is not the Adirondack Mountains; this is a very flat county with orchards and dairy farming. But, during the period from 1975 to 1985, trapping was very profitable. Fur prices were at their peak, with muskrats bringing as high as $7 - $9 a piece, raccoon $55, red fox $90, and eastern coyote $60. These prices brought out the criminal element. I was constantly checking muskrat trap lines in the state game management area for violations such as placing a trap within 5 feet of a muskrat house, operating another person's traps without his permission, not visiting traps once every 24 hours, and not having name tags on the traps.

I was a muskrat trapper before I was an environmental conservation officer, so I knew how these guys thought. I enjoyed working a trap line. I would carry an old army-surplus shoulder bag that contained my short-handle axe and a long rubber glove that would extend to my shoulder. I would wait until the ice had frozen thick enough for me to walk on and with that, I was off across the marsh.

Muskrats lived either in the banks of the waterway or in houses they made out of cattails. The law said you could not place a trap within five feet of a muskrat house but, when there was money to be made, the temptation was great and sometimes trappers would take chances. Muskrats were plentiful and a good trapper could catch 20 to 30 in a day. At an average of $8 each, that was a very profitable day. With fur prices this high, trapping was more than a recreation, it was a business.

But, for these guys, the thrill wasn't just the skill of placing a trap successfully; the real thrill was competing and catching more than the other guy. For instance, if I knew Ben Riley caught 39 for the day, then I had to catch 40. So, to do that, some trappers would cut corners and stretch the law. But, the fraternity of trappers would feel justified in giving me a phone call when other trappers had not been checking his traps or was not using name tags.

When a trapper had 50 to 100 traps set, it could be difficult to keep track and locate every one. To do this, trappers would put a 5 to 8 foot long stick next to each trap with a piece of colored yarn wrapped around the top. The yarn could be red, blue, yellow or whatever material the trapper had an abundance of, as long as it was a different color from the trapper who was trapping around you.

Stealing traps was common. Traps were expensive, ranging from $3 each for a 110 Conibear up to $7.50 each for a 220 Conibear. Conibear traps were a new body-gripping trap that would grab the animal if it swam into the trigger and would drown it. But, the older style leg-hold trap that had been used for centuries was also still very common.

I found trappers to be very hearty individuals. One particular story comes to mind. It was 1984 and I had decided it was time to check muskrat trap lines in the Tonawanda Game Management Area. The temperature had been below freezing for over a week and the ice was quite thick. After parking the car, I grabbed my trapping bag with its small axe and trapping glove and headed towards the dike. What a day! The wind was blowing strongly, bringing in a squall. One hundred yards ahead I saw what I thought was a person walking towards me. He looked like a human snowman. There couldn't have been more difference in the way the two of us were dressed. I had on my insulated winter coat, gloves, a scarf, and a cap with earflaps pulled down over my ears. He was not wearing a hat and his coat was hanging open with his hairy chest exposed to the elements.

Barney Jones was one especially interesting trapper. A big, burly man, he belonged in the era with the mountain men. I used to pick certain days when I knew the ice would be over two inches thick to check the nametags on any traps I could find. I would grab my ax, put on my rubber gloves and long johns, an insulated winter coat and a hat with pull-down flaps and I was ready to walk the marsh. I felt nice and cozy. Frequently I would look up and see an apparition appearing through a whiteout of snow. Even at a distance of over 150 yards I knew it was Bernie. He was not wearing a hat and his coat was always unbuttoned at the neck and his hairy chest was hanging out of the open coat. His hair was blowing in the wind and his face and hair were all covered with snow. I was covered from head to toe and Bernie was sauntering along like it was a walk in the park.

We would talk about making sure he visited his traps every 24 hours and I would always end by asking him,

"Hi, Bo, aren't you cold?"

"Na."

"Let's check a few of your traps."

Everything checked out fine, but I will never forget the sight of that trapper without a hat, his hair and face coated with snow and his coat hanging open in the midst of a snowstorm. What a sight! Trappers were tough characters!

The Trappers

What a great career I had. But, it would have been just another job if it had not been for the many interesting people I met along the way. Some you can group into categories, others just stand alone in their uniqueness. But, they all found a way to put a smile on my face.

Trappers were a very unique group. I was fortunate to have been an officer in a county where the muskrat was king. I not only had a six-thousand-acre game management area, but also numerous ditches and creeks that all held muskrats. During the 1970s and through the 1980s trapped muskrats were bringing as much as $9 each. Some of these trappers were so good that they turned it into a full time occupation. I always respected the trappers, because I felt I was one of them. I was brought up as a kid trapping muskrats in a ditches and creeks. For those of you who have never done it I say, don't knock it unless you have tried it.

I would rate Elliott Harmon as one of the three best outdoorsmen I ever knew. He was an excellent trapper of all species and could catch a fox as easily as a mink. Trapping was his life; he was a professional. Elliott would always try to trip me up with his questions but I don't think it ever worked. I think we respected each other. I knew he was a hell of a trapper and he knew I could be anywhere out there at anytime. That was the impression I wanted to leave with these trappers, that I was always prepared, no matter the weather. And, even the "professionals" can slip up once in awhile. I had to be ready.

I had seen Elliott's truck parked off the Bartell Road for the past couple of days and was headed for where I believed his trap line was. He would always mark his stakes with a blue piece of thread, making it easier to find his traps. The third trip in I found a beaver in one of his 220 Conibear traps. I checked the tag to make sure it belonged to Elliott. Leaving the beaver in place, I put a metal seal with my number up the beaver's rectum in case I had to leave the scene before he got there to check his traps. I quickly got in my vehicle and proceeded about 100 yards to an abandoned driveway. Backing in, I had a good view of anyone entering the marsh and sat back to wait.

An hour went by, then two, then three. I'm thinking, *Come on, Elliott, hurry up and get here.* I never knew him to miss a day checking his traps so I felt confident he would show up. A car passed me going in the opposite direction filled with what looked like hunters. They went around a small curve in the road and I saw the brake lights come on. Three men in orange jackets and a beagle got out of the 1985 Dodge van. It would only take me a minute to give these guys a look-see. I quickly drove over, exited my patrol car and walked over to them. They were out to do a little rabbit hunting. Their licenses checked out fine, so I thanked them and was quickly back behind the wheel, headed back to my hiding spot. And, there was Elliott Harmon's truck. I hurried up behind it and jumped out just as Elliott was about to pull away.

"Elliott, let's check your fur for the day."

Twelve muskrats and one beaver.

"Elliott, you caught that beaver right here."

"No I didn't."

I reached down to the beaver and pulled the seal out of its butt.

"Well then, Elliott, what is this? I'll tell you what it is. It's my metal seal with my number 24 on it that I inserted into the beaver this morning. Here is your ticket for taking a beaver out of season."

This time my patience paid off.

***

In closing, I cannot forget my friend, Raymond "Ike" James, from Somerset.

Our friendship started in the late 1970s when I decided to raise hogs. Ike had an ad in the local newspaper, "Little pigs for sale." The price seemed fair, so I decided to call on him. His pigs were Diracs and were red in color. I bought a dozen of them for $15 each and that started our friendship.

Ike was in his late sixty's when I met him, stood five-feet-eight inches tall, and always had a smile on his face. But, what made him stand out was his voice, which was very gravelly and distinctive. Even if I could not see him, if I heard that voice, I knew it was Ike. Over the next ten years I enjoyed listening to Ike's outdoor stories about hunting pheasants and deer and trapping muskrats. He operated a farm part-time and had worked for the New York State Department of Transportation until he retired at age 65 so he could devote more time to his hunting, fishing and trapping.

One hot summer day in 1981 I received a call from Ike telling me a Great Horned Owl was killing his ducks and wanting to know what I was going to do about it. I proceeded to tell him that all hawks and owls are federal and state protected.

"You cannot shoot them, Ike. Can you put the ducks in your barn for a few days until the owl decides they're gone?"

"Okay, okay, I'll try it."

Four days went by and I was hoping the owl had disappeared. Ike called me again to tell me he had let the ducks out. Another week went by and I got call from Ike telling me the owl had returned.

"Okay, Ike, let's try it one more time, but this time let's put the ducks in the barn for two weeks and we'll see what happens."

Then, two weeks later Ike let the ducks out, and the next day I received a call from him telling me the owl was back. So, I went over to his place and checked things out. There was the owl.

Thank God Ike was not overly upset.

I was able to corner the owl, throw my jacket over it, and transport it to the far side of wildlife refuge.

Then, weeks went by and no call from Ike. I was not sure I wanted to know what happened to that owl. No one else called me, so I never asked.

At the age of seventy Ike was now teaching himself to trap fox. Why? Because fur prices were going out of sight. A red fox pelt could bring between $50 to $80 each! And boy! Could Ike catch them. He also took a lot of pride in skinning and fleshing his fox. One 25-degree day in January I stopped in to hear his latest fox story. He was working on skinning a red fox and I noticed there were large pieces of fur missing on its back legs.

"Ike, why did you skin that red fox that way?" In his distinct voice he said,

"The fur was all gone; I think it had the mange."

"Throw it away Ike; it's not worth catching the mange."

"Oh, I won't catch it."

"Okay, good luck."

Two weeks later I decided to call on Ike again and see what was new. I knocked on the door and he motioned for me to come in. Right away he said,

"I did it, I caught the mange."

"Oh boy, tell me about it."

It seems that every time he came into the house he would start itching and scratching and then he went to bed and gave it to his wife, who was not happy to get it. All the two of them had been doing for the past two weeks was washing sheets and applying prescription medicine to their bodies.

Dick & Trapper Fred Weisman, mid-1980s

Were You Ever Assaulted?

Yes, I was, and the memory continues to come back to me. It wasn't with a gun, it wasn't with a knife. It was with a vehicle. During my 34-year career, I always did what my gut reaction told me to do. I guess it was the right reaction, because I'm still here to tell my story. I did not want to be a dead hero, so when I was dealing with known criminals I would always make a habit of finding another officer to accompany me to confront the violator.

This particular time, Columbus Day 1976, was a holiday for many school children and the start of a new phenomenon for fishermen in New York State. There were huge salmon and trout in streams that had never seen fish runs before. It was in the newspapers and on television: huge 30-pound fish were proceeding from Lake Ontario in Olcott to a dam in

18-Mile Creek. It created a gold-rush mentality that I don't think anyone could have anticipated. Fishing regulations were very liberal; snagging and night fishing were acceptable, with a limit of five fish per day. What more could you ask for? On this Columbus Day, it had rained during the night, and was cool, with a temperature of 48 degrees. I had a feeling it was a good day to catch a fish or a fisherman.

Dick with a salmon, early 1980s

As I approached the area of the Burt Dam, I could not believe my eyes. There were cars everywhere, hundreds of them, parked along the highway, on private property, wherever they could cram them. It was a mass of cars and fishermen. I parked my marked green sedan in among a group of trucks at the top of the hill. Walking down the trail, I felt very inadequate. There were at least three hundred to five hundred fishermen here. What a sight! I tried to blend in with the crowd. I had my cover jacket on, which covered my pistol and my uniform shirt and my rubber boots covered my green work pants. I had taken my badge out of my pocket and put it in my cover jacket where it would be easy to get to. Mentally I was in my searching mode. I never looked directly at any one fisherman, I was checking five guys down the line, taking mental notes of what they looked like and what they were wearing. The atmosphere was quite eerie. Except for the water coming over the dam, the lack of noise was deafening.

I had no particular reason for choosing the two men I did, I just decided it was time to start checking for license violations and I was going to start with these two snaggers. I pulled my badge out and, at the same time, said,

"Conservation Officer, Dick Lang. May I check your fishing license please?"

On this occasion, I used my polite, soft-spoken voice, not my loud authoritarian one. These two individuals quickly owned up to the fact that they did not have a current fishing license. In a soft voice I told them where to stand while I checked others. Repeating myself, I said,

"Stand right here and don't move."

After checking three more fishermen, I had a feeling something wasn't the way I wanted it to be. The two fishermen were gone. I saw them running up the embankment to their vehicle. Jamming the expired licenses of the last two fishermen into my coat pocket I yelled,

"I will contact you later."

All the fishermen stopped what they were doing to watch me chase those two guys up the hill. As we were running I was yelling,

"Stop! Conservation Officer, you are under arrest."

That did not seem to bother them. They never looked back, never said a word, they just kept running. As I cleared the top of the bank, I saw them slamming the doors on a beat up black van. I quickly went to the passenger door and pulled on the latch. It was locked.

"Open the door," I yelled.

The passenger was inches from my face but he refused to look at me, continuing to look straight ahead. All of a sudden, the driver started the motor and, as the van started motoring down the highway, I held on, continuing to yell,

"Stop! Conservation Officer."

No reaction on the part of these two men. In moments we were proceeding south on Route 78. Speed was becoming critical and I decided I better let go and get the license plate number. These two are nuts. All this for a six dollar and twenty-five cent fishing license! I needed that license plate number. Well, here goes, let's hope I can get a good plate number. I looked and, sure enough, it was nice and clean, a lot better than the condition of the van. I quickly ran to my vehicle and wrote down the number. I radioed to the local state police station to be on the lookout for a black van with the New York plate -----. All the police agencies were taking part in the search, but those two gave me a momentary slip.

It wasn't long and I was at the home of my local Newfane Town Justice Wilburt Rathke. By now I had the name and address of the owner of the van, which added a new twist to the charges; the van came back unregistered and uninsured. Well, well, that just added to the fun of hunting these two down. Let's see now, fishing charges, Penal Law, and vehicle and traffic. I felt very confident as I proceeded to obtain my arrest warrant. I needed another officer to accompany me. Like I said, let's not be a hero, let's just get our man. I contacted Environmental Conservation Officer Jim Groebe, to assist me.

"Jim, I had a guy try and run me over this morning. Could you assist me in serving an arrest warrant on him?"

"Sure Dick, let's meet around 7:00 PM at the State Police Station on the Thruway. See you at seven."

With all my paper work in order, I met Officer Groebe at the designated location at 7:00 PM. Filling him in on the details we proceeded to the location. Sure enough, there was the van we were looking for. So far so good. Knock, Knock. A moment went by before a young boy came to the door, a boy too young to know how to lie yet.

"Hi, I would like to see Fred Embers."

The boy turned and yelled, "Daddy there is someone here to see you."

I could hear his footsteps approaching and I was more than ready to arrest this smart guy.

"Mr. Embers, you are under arrest. Get your shoes on."

I followed him into the house.

"How did you find me? How did you find me?" was all he kept saying.

Shoes on, I had him handcuffed, gave him his Miranda Warning, explained the charges against him and walked him to my state car. It was not the way I wanted his son to see him, but I was not taking any chances after he tried to run me over. I radioed the State Police asking them to please make a call to Judge Rathke, telling him we were on our way. Within thirty minutes we were at Judge Rathke's office and ushered the defendant in to face the charges. After reading the charges, bail was set and, since he was unable to post bail, he went off to cool his heels at the Niagara County Jail. He just kept repeating,

"How did you find me?"

Never a dull moment in the life of a conservation officer.

Hunting While Intoxicated

It was the first Saturday of the duck season in October of 1977 and the weather was beautiful. The sky was a brilliant shade of blue, filled with high, puffy white clouds. The air was crisp and clean, and I could smell the musty, colored leaves that crunched underfoot. Earlier in the day I had worked the Tonawanda Wildlife Area checking waterfowl hunters, finding no violations. Jack Hassett, conservation officer from Erie County, was scheduled to work with me that evening. At 5:00 PM Jack showed up at my home where he left his state car and rode with me to check duck hunters.

I enjoyed Jack, even though he was old enough to be my father. In his dress uniform, ramrod straight at 6'2" and smoking a pipe, he was a model conservation officer. He had been the game warden in my hometown when I was growing up and everyone who hunted feared him. Now I was working with him as an equal. What a change!

Jack and I got along very well. He enjoyed working the swamp with me and I enjoyed spending time with him. He was responsible for my nickname of Pintail, a puddle duck. Leaving my headquarters, we laid out our plan, deciding where I would drop him off and what time I would pick him up. In case he found a violation, I gave him a list of the judges in the town of Royalton. We were both dressed in hunting clothes and hip boots and carried a shotgun, so we would look like the other hunters. I dropped Jack off on a west dike and told him I would see him shortly after sunset. He nodded, grabbed his shotgun and hat and said,

"See you later, Pintail." And off he went.

I drove to the other end of the same dike and parked next to two other cars. I grabbed my cover coat, shotgun and hat and headed west on the dike, looking and listening for hunters. Suddenly, I spotted two of them about fifty yards in front of me. Walking closer, I saw some beer cans on the ground, eight of them, some full, some empty. This could be interesting! The men were hunkered down in the cattails wearing only low-cut leather boots, not good enough for the swamps. Walking up to them I asked,

"How are the ducks flying?"

"Thousands, there are thousands of them," one of them replied.

I knew there was a new state law that just went into effect, hunting while intoxicated, and thought, *Hey, these two just might fit the bill.*

I walked past the two of them about fifty yards, sat down along the dike and played hunter while I watched them. They did not shoot, just sat there throwing their cans in the marsh. Well, at least I could get them for littering.

All of a sudden they stood up, gathered their gear and started towards their vehicle. I stood up, checked my watch and found it to be well before closing time. Well, here goes. This is a new law, I hope I get it right. As we got to the cars I said,

"Conservation Officer Dick Lang, and I think you boys were hunting while intoxicated."

I read them their rights, made sure their guns were unloaded and placed the guns in my trunk. I locked their car and we all got into my patrol car and headed to the Wrights Corners State Police Barracks. Calling ahead, I informed the radio operator about two individuals suspected of hunting while intoxicated and asked if they had a trooper at the station who could administer a breathalyzer test for me. The word came back that they did and I told them we'd be there within thirty minutes. I have to admit, I was driving rather fast, as I had no idea how fast the alcohol would wear off.

I pulled into the circular driveway and escorted them up the stairs and into the office. We met the sergeant on duty who put them in a room where the trooper administrated the test. A short time later the word came back that they both had met the criteria for hunting while intoxicated.

Now I had some phone calls to make, first to Lt. Bob Kauffman to give him the details of my new arrest. Then I called the men's wives, explaining what they had done and where to come and pick them up, since they were not allowed to drive. The poor ladies had no idea where Wrights Corners was. We could have been on the moon for all they knew, but finally a vehicle pulled into the station with the two women aboard. I informed them that their husbands had been issued two tickets each and where and when the court date was. I would not have wanted to be riding in that car on the way back!

My partner was still sitting by himself out in the swamp, two hours after the time I said I would pick him up. With no way to reach him, I was worried about his reaction. Pulling into the designated parking spot I saw him sitting on a chain link fence. *Oh boy, was I in trouble.* I immediately started to tell him my story. And you know what? He never got mad at me. Heaving a sigh of relief, I asked if he'd found any violations.

"No," he said. "But I still enjoyed myself. It was a beautiful night."

The Fox in the Sun Porch

It was a hot Wednesday in July when I received a complaint from a lady who said she had an injured fox. I knew where it was, just off the Carmen Road, in the village of Middleport. I pulled into the driveway, exited the car and headed towards a screened-in porch.

At the same time, a lady came out a side door speaking in a low voice,

"Mr. Lang? Mr. Lang, the fox is in there," she said, pointing to the screened-in porch.

"How did it get in there?"

"Well, about four o'clock yesterday afternoon I was coming home from work when a fox ran out in front of a car and got hit. I love foxes and I felt so bad for it that I just had to stop and see if it was hurt. It was dazed and I did not know if anything else was broken so I picked it up and put it in my car and drove it home."

"You didn't pick it up with your bare hands, did you?" Now I was irritated. "Let me get this straight. You picked up a fox that had been hit by a car with no protective gloves on?!"

"Yes, I love foxes."

"Well, you better hope the fox was not carrying rabies. If the Health Department determines it was, then you will have to receive a series of the rabies vaccine. But, it's all up to the Niagara County Health Department."

She opened the door to the porch and the first thing to hit me was the strong smell of fox urine. Wow, what a smell. Fox urine in a very small room, on a very hot day. It was enough to knock me over. Then I noticed a beautiful red fox hiding behind the sofa. We were wasting time. I had to make some decisions and I had to make them quickly, as I had to be at our monthly law-enforcement meeting at Rushford Lake in an hour and a half. I called the Health Department.

"Hi Jack, this is Dick Lang from the DEC. I'll tell you what I have."

After hearing my story they agreed to pick up the fox but only after I had "dispatched" it. No problem. I removed the .357 ammunition from my gun and replaced it with .357 birdshot. Entering the porch, I was within inches of the animal when I dispatched that smelly red fox. My parting words to the woman were,

"The Health Department is on its way and they will test its brain for any signs of the virus. Next time, please keep your hands off injured wildlife."

The Hartland Chase

In the fall of 1982, one of the challenges of being an environmental conservation officer was controlling the spotlighting of deer. If I saw a spotlighter, I always had to ask myself whether it is simply a family out showing the kids the deer, or is it a poacher out to get an early deer for his freezer?

One crisp November night I was settling in for the evening when the phone rang.

"Mr. Lang, there is a car on Town Line Road, between Quaker Road and Peet Street. They've been shining a light and I believe I heard a shot."

"I'll be right there," I replied to the caller.

Making a right turn off Quaker Road, I saw a car on the north side of the road and quickly made a U-turn, pulling up behind it. The car was empty, but shining my hand-held light, I saw a spotlight and shells scattered about the front seat. Hearing voices, I quickly jotted down the license plate and backed into an abandoned driveway where I had a good view of the vehicle.

Within ten minutes I noticed shadows approaching the vehicle. With the lights off, I pulled up right next to the car. The two men jumped in the souped-up Dodge and, with that, we were off like the Dukes of Hazard. We turned west on Town Line Road and they proceeded to pull away from me like I was standing still. I placed a call to the State Police requesting a car and asked if they would contact Environmental Conservation Officer Neil Ross for assistance. It did not take long for those deerjackers to lose me, since their car had a lot more power than my official car. But, I felt confident that I had enough information to apprehend them.

Officer Ross and I spent hours circling the area and checking residences and driveways waiting for the vehicle to return. At 2:15 am, I drove past the home of his parents, and saw the vehicle in question. The house was dark, giving the appearance that nothing had happened for many hours. Officer Ross stood by the vehicle as I proceeded to knock on the door. Finally, Joel Gray came to the door. I told him,

"Joel, come outside. I have some questions for you. Open your car trunk."

I could see where they had been working hard to remove the deer blood and hair, but I've done this many times. It's not hard to locate traces of blood and hair when you know how.

"Joel, I know where you shot the deer. Where is it?" Joel wasn't in the mood to cooperate, but I can play hard ball too. "Joel, I'll have to seize the car as evidence until I can get the case resolved." That got his attention. "What do you mean? I won't have a car to drive."

"That's correct. The tow truck driver will hold the vehicle as evidence."

He still wasn't cooperating. Since all I needed to prosecute the case was blood and hair, I issued a ticket for the illegal taking of a deer and the vehicle and traffic violations were turned over to the State Police for prosecution. The car was towed away as evidence and was held for five days. By the end of the week, the defendant had settled for a $502.50 fine plus storage charges, which amounted to $35 a day for five days. In this case, my perseverance paid off.

Dick 2003

Dogs Chasing Deer

During my first twenty years as a conservation officer we were constantly receiving complaints of domestic dogs chasing deer. Since the 1990s, it's not as much of a problem, but from the 1960s through the 1980s it was a common complaint. Dad would go off to work and let the dog out and the dog would hunt and harass anything from domestic animals to the white-tailed deer. In the dog's defense, every dog is a natural hunter. Given the chance, they will all chase; it is their instinct to hunt.

Many complaints were received from deer hunters who had been on watch, patiently waiting for their chance to shoot a mature buck. Finally they would see one as he came crashing through the brush with his tongue hanging out of his mouth, his eyes wide with fear and a dog on his heels. Whether it was a single dog or a group of dogs, the deer was running for its life. To put it in track terms, the deer is a sprinter, the dog is a long-distance runner. It was just a matter of time before the dog caught the deer. If the hunter was fed up with what he had seen, he would call me and I would have him sign a supporting deposition as to what he had witnessed. Many times the witness knew who owned the dogs.

The Conservation Law stated that conservation officers, state police, forest rangers and other named police officers could shoot a dog in the act of chasing deer. The last thing I wanted to do was shoot someone's dog. I would much rather hit them in the wallet with a $200 fine.

As the 1980s were ending, I noticed that the dog-chasing-deer complaints were all but gone. I think there were a few reasons for this. The time of the hunting dog had all but disappeared. As the pheasant and grouse populations were greatly reduced, people thought, why keep a dog? Finally, dogs can be very expensive to own, so most people felt that if they were going to put a substantial amount of money into a pet, they would keep better control of it.

A Cougar in the Car

I knew I was in the wild animal business and that
there would be some unusual cases, but a few of them
really stuck in my memory. One started in the
Lockport Town Court on a Tuesday night. I had
issued a ticket to a gruff, fifty-six-year-old for
possessing a ferret without a permit. While in court,
the defendant got rather indignant saying,

"This seems pretty foolish, writing me a ticket for
this little ferret. Why don't you go after the guy with
the cougar?"

"What guy?"

"The guy on Tonawanda Creek Road, Town of
Clarence. He has a cougar."

"Are you sure? Do you know what a cougar is?"

"Yes, I know what a cougar is. It's a cougar."

The following day we had a law enforcement meeting in Buffalo. I brought the information up to my lieutenant and the conservation officer in charge of that area. After the meeting, Officers Keppner and Becker and I went to the home in question. Sure enough, we could see the cougar in a corncrib, visible right from the road. We were shocked. We drove up to a very well maintained white farmhouse with a red barn and a large corncrib. Knocking on the door, we were met by a short, middle-aged, round-faced man.

"Yes, can I help you?"

We identified ourselves as state conservation officers and stated we were there on a complaint of possession of a cougar.

"Yea, I have a cougar. I bought it in Ohio two months ago."

"Do you have a New York State Permit to possess this cougar?"

"No, I was going to get it. I heard you get it after you buy the animal."

The cougar was only six months old and had been purchased in Ohio at an auction. The animal had its claws and fangs removed and it seemed to be very friendly. Mr. Lawson invited us into his home, where I saw many large pictures of cougars. This man seemed to have an obsession with them.

Dick and the cougar, circa 1980

Officer Becker informed Lawson that we were going to seize the animal. We had picked up a large cage from the game farm and we were ready to transport it. The defendant felt we could not give the animal the right care and felt it should be left with him. No deal.

The cougar was transported by state wildlife personal and taken to the John White Game Farm in the town of Alabama, where the state raised pheasants. Since the facility was not designed to house a cougar, it was put in a locked barn. The next day I checked on the animal and found numerous people watching it and enjoying themselves, since most of them had only ever seen a cougar in books.

The following morning the cougar was to be transported by wildlife personnel to the Utica Zoo. Morning came early; my phone rang at 6:30 AM. It was Dan Carroll, the wildlife biologist in charge of the area.

"Dick, the cougar is gone."

"What do you mean, the cougar is gone?"

"Someone came in with a crowbar, took the door off the building and took the cougar."

Only one name came to mind, Sam Lawson, the person who started this whole mess. He seemed obsessed with the animal. I contacted Environmental Conservation Officer Harold Keppner, and the New York State Police and told them to meet me at the defendant's house. After much questioning, Mr. Lawson showed us where he had taken the cougar. It was chained to a bush about one hundred and fifty yards behind his home. This time he was arrested by the state police for criminal trespass and other charges.

After a few pictures, we put the cougar in the back seat of our state car. Officer Keppner and I drove east on the New York State Thruway to meet the wildlife staff from Utica.

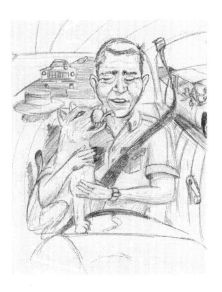

What an exciting trip it was, with a cougar in the backseat looking out the windows of the car, peering at the faces in the passing trucks and cars.

Those other passengers were sure surprised to see a cougar free in the back of our car. After about an hour on the thruway, we were glad to meet the biologist who would be taking the cougar to the Utica Zoo.

December 1969
Bob Kauffman, Everett Larkin

The Skeleton

It was a bright sunny morning, the day after
Halloween, and my job had me patrolling for
waterfowl hunters in the Tonawanda Wildlife Area. I
was on a paved road without any houses and kept
glancing ahead for any vehicles parked in concealed
areas. Rounding a curve, I noticed an old, full-size
Chevrolet backed into an abandoned driveway.
Looking more closely, I noticed a young man seated
behind the wheel. Stopping my patrol car, I
approached the vehicle cautiously. Our conversation
went something like this:

"Hi. Are you doing any hunting?"

No, just listening to the radio."

"Aren't you supposed to be in school?"

"No, I dropped out."

"Any guns in the vehicle?"

"No."

"Would you please open your trunk for me?"

"Yea, sure."

With that, he put the key in the lock, the trunk opened wide and I jumped back with a start. There, looking back at me, was a full-size human skeleton. I could not believe my eyes. In a rather shaky voice, I asked,

"Where did you get that?"

He said he got it from a friend.

"Is your friend in school?"

"No."

But I still felt he got it from a school. I asked for his driver's license. Putting him and the skeleton in my patrol car, we proceeded to a phone at the state game facility where I called the high school in question. Telling the secretary I was Dick Lang, a New York State Environmental Conservation Officer, I asked her to check and see if the school was missing a skeleton. She was gone about 15 minutes. When she returned she told me,

"Yes we are. It's missing from a closet in the biology room."

"Well, I am quite sure I have it," I replied.

I gave the office the boy's name and was told he was a full-time student shown absent for the day.

"I'll bring him down with the skeleton," I told her.

"What were you going to do with it?" I asked the student.

"We were going to hang it from some trees in the center of town, but we got scared and never took it out of the trunk."

As I pulled into the school parking lot, I could see the secretary waiting for us.

"Officer Lang, I will show you to the principal's office."

Proceeding down the hall a short distance I could see the principal waiting in front of his office.

"Officer Lang, I'll take care of this."

And with that he reached up, grabbed the student by the ear, pulled him into the office, and slammed the door shut behind them.

That was one of those situations you never forgot.

The Name Change Game

It was late August, 1982 when I received a call telling me that Mac Elliott was shooting deer and selling them to the migrant farm workers to be used as wild goat meat. Where was this going on? Newfane, Appleton, and Burt, usually at night but not always.

On Tuesday, September 4th, while patrolling a dirt road in the town of Newfane, I glanced at the road in front of the car and saw rifle casings shining back at me. Stopping the patrol car, I saw five .22 long rifle spent shells shining in the sun. There were some apple tote boxes on the north side of the road and apple trees all around. Walking to the nearest box, I looked in and, to my amazement, saw a small doe deer. Pulling it out of the box I found a .22 hole in the deer. Suddenly, I heard Federal Officer Dan Smoot come on the radio. I called his car number and he said he would be at my location within fifteen minutes.

When Dan arrived, I explained the situation and suggested we dig around and see if we could find any lead. We dug out a .22 long rifle casing. This case was starting to look real good. We took pictures, made notes, cataloged the casings from the road and removed the deer. We felt we had a suspect, but needed to do a few interviews. This was fun. I called on Charlie Shepperd, who ran a little fruit stand and was a country preacher.

"Charlie, what do you know about Mac Elliott selling deer to people in your congregation?"

"Yes," he replied, "that did happen, but those families are no longer in the area."

Charlie said he had seen Mac with a gun. It was a bolt action, clip feed, not in very good shape. Mac's legal residence was still at his parents' place, so I made up a search warrant for their home in the village of Newfane.

I called Officer Vosburg to assist me in serving the search warrant. When he arrived, I gave him the lowdown on what I was looking for. We arrived at Elliott's house at 4:15 PM and knocked on the door. A Sam Elliott came to the door.

"Can I help you?"

We identified ourselves as Conservation Officers Dick Lang, and Kimpton Vosburg and explained we were there to execute a search warrant. Elliott said to his wife,

"Lang's here and he wants to search for a gun."

Kimp made small talk with the family while I searched for the gun. I looked around the house and found some shotguns, but no .22 rifle. Then I looked behind the couch in the living room and there was a disassembled .22 barrel.

"Where is the rest of the gun?" I asked the parents.

"I don't know. You'll have to find it."

I went into the dining room and looked behind the china cabinet and found the rest of the rifle. The parents were given a receipt and a copy of the search warrant and we left without incident. Boy was I excited. What a case! I really felt good. This was my first hard-core investigation and it was going to lead to an arrest warrant.

The next morning I was at the typewriter making out my application for the arrest warrant. Paper work complete, I was off to Judge Rathke in Newfane. He approved my paperwork and signed the warrant. The word was out on the street, Lang had an arrest warrant for Mac Elliott for taking a deer during the closed season.

On a Tuesday night the phone rang and a voice asked,

"Hi Dick, are still looking for Mac?"

I said, "Well, if you're talking about Mac Elliott, yes I am."

"Well, he's at his house up next to the dam right now."

"I'll be right there."

I made two phone calls, one to the Wrights Corners State Police and the other to Captain David Schultz, who was a captain of our investigation unit. Prior to Captain Schultz becoming an environmental conservation officer, he had been an investigator with the Niagara County Sheriff's Department. During that time, he had a Mr. Elliott as an informant. I had kept Captain Schultz informed of my case as it progressed and I updated him now.

"Dave, a witness saw Elliott at his home in Newfane moments ago. Could you come and talk to him if need be?"

"Sure Dick, I'll meet you there in thirty minutes."

We met a short distance from the residence, two troopers, the captain and me. We left our cars and proceeded quickly to the house, one trooper and myself to the front door and the captain and the other trooper to the back door. Knocking on the door, I identified myself. We could hear lots of noise from inside, doors closing, footsteps going from room to room, along with quiet voices. It was a small one-story house, which made it easy to cover. After much pounding on my part, his wife finally opened the door just a crack.

"Yes, what do you want?"

"Dick Lang, Conservation Officer, and I have an arrest warrant for Mac. I know he is here, so have him come out or we're coming in."

He didn't come out, so we went in. Using our flashlights, we searched from room to room. I shined my light into a spare bedroom that was full of boxes. At first glance I didn't see anything, but when I directed my light into the closet, there was a big naked belly sticking out between two boxes.

"Mac, come out of there easy. Keep your hands where I can see them."

He was no problem. Mac had a deep voice, and was slightly overweight, and when he came out from under those boxes it was quite a sight. He only had his undershorts on. I was glad to see he was going to cooperate. After he dressed, I handcuffed him, and off we went to the town hall.

Judge Joseph Slomba was there to meet us. Mac pleaded not guilty and was released on $500 bail. The court date came and went and no Elliott. He was getting under my skin. I knew he was a truck driver, so I was always on the lookout for him. The second court date came and still no Mac. I had his bail revoked and another arrest warrant issued with bail at $1,000. Two months went by and I got a call from Mac.

"Hey Lang, can you reduce that bail?"

"Mac, I am going to be around a long time and I will catch you."

Next, I went to the local New York State Police Station and had them put the arrest warrant on the all-state pick up. That resulted in a call from the Illinois State Police. They had stopped him in Joliet, Illinois on a traffic violation and wanted to know if I wanted to come to Illinois and pick him up. I said no, my department would not let me go out of state. So they released him.

Four months went by and I received another phone call from Elliott asking if his dad came over and paid the fine would that take care of it. I told him that it would, but that the fine was still $1,000. The next day I received a radio message to call the court clerk in Newfane. I was in the area so I stopped by the court. Mac's dad had just left and had paid the full amount. I felt good. The case took some time but I was proud of the way I had proceeded with it.

My Open Letter to a Conservation Officer

In 1969 I started the job of my dreams. I was 28 years old, full of energy, excitement, and enthusiasm, wanting to learn everything I could as fast as possible. I felt that the career of a conservation officer really suited me, it fit my personality.

In my fourth year as a conservation officer I still could not wait to get up in the morning and start the day. Every day was different; what more could I ask for? By this time I had started to hear grumbling from some of the older officers regarding pay, hours worked, equipment, complaints, the phone ringing, or "the lieutenant is looking for you." I never fell into the trap of not wanting to answer my complaints. I loved being a conservation officer. Every day I looked forward to putting on my green uniform and representing the Conservation Department in the marked state patrol car.

In November of 1975 I was checking duck hunters in the Tonawanda Wildlife Management Area when a complaint came across the radio of a possible illegal pheasant shooting. The officer involved was less than enthusiastic and possibly did not give the complaint his best effort.

Later that night I wrote a letter to myself as if I was writing to another officer. I finished my letter, but it was always near me. It was at the bottom of my clipboard, which sat next to me in my patrol car. At the end of my 34-year career I still lived by that open letter. I still had the excitement. I still had the enthusiasm.

Thank you New York State for giving me my dream job.

Here's the letter:

Do you still get out of bed in the morning thinking *Thank God for the great job I have*, like you used to do when you first came on as a conservation officer? Or do you now get up in the morning and complain about how bad they have treated you?

Are you stuck in a rut or do you still look at each new day with expectation and excitement?

Do you still have imagination and initiative or do you like to overstay your stops in the coffee shop?

Are you honestly able to look at your patrol techniques and see if your patrol is producing results?

The Size of the Officer

Conservation officers really come in all sizes but
sometimes it seemed that in order to be hired you had
to be big and tough. In the early years, game laws and
game protectors were not always held in high regard
and that could result in officers being assaulted.
Many officers patrolled by foot or by boat in remote
areas where a fellow officer was far away. So, the
bigger you were the bigger the image you projected.
Especially in the early years, what seemed to stand
out was how huge these men were. It seemed that a
basic criterion for being hired was to be 6'2" tall and
250 pounds At 6 feet and 160 pounds, I felt small.
Add to their size the uniform they wore, the Stetson
hat, the pants with the black stripe, the green jacket
with the wool collar and the gun, and these men
seemed larger than life. They had an imposing aura
about them that you felt the minute you encountered

them. And, the stories that circulated only gave them greater mystique.

It seemed some people had to try to convince themselves they were as "big" as the conservation officers. On one occasion I was told by an individual who had been trapping muskrats that he had outrun Officer Vosburg while checking his traps. Now, I knew Officer Vosburg kept himself in great shape and I simply told him that if Vosburg had wanted to catch him, he would have. That's all there was to it.

A similar situation involved a by-gone officer, Lank O'Brian. It always made me laugh to hear the stories.

"You know, my friend threw Lank O'Brian in Oak Orchard Creek."

"Your buddy must have been a very big guy."

"No, he's 5 feet 9 inches and 170 pounds."

"Well, Lank is 6'6" tall and 280 pounds. Do you really believe that happened? I don't know why you would believe such crap."

There were a lot of people who claimed to have thrown O'Bee in every creek in Orleans County, but I never found any of them.

But, generally, our imposing presence seemed to impress the public. I always liked to hear their stories.

"I saw you up in that helicopter going over the swamp."

"Yea, that was me."

I never let them know that I hated small planes and had never flown in a helicopter. But you always let them believe you were everywhere. But, sometimes, even I couldn't hide. When it came to checking fishermen on the Olcott Pier I was a marked man. Even if I wasn't wearing my Class A dress uniform, I would just hear them say,

"Here comes Lang, get your license out."

They simply recognized me from the way I walked. Everyone has his unique way of walking and I had mine. I never could hide it.

2008
Retired Officers in our living room
Front row: Jerry Sporer, Morris McCargo,
Gene Tuohey, Al Riegel, Smiling Dick
Back row: Don Becker, Gary Bobseine,
Dennis Praczkajlo, Chuck Robishaw, Doug Case,
Jim Rackl, Dan Ward, Dave Schultz

Class A Uniform

When I first started my job, I learned a lot from the older experienced officers. One of the most important things I learned was to stagger my starting and ending time. I learned to leave home at different times, take different routes and, in general, to appear unpredictable. I wanted to keep the violators guessing as to where I would be and at what time. If I was going out in my Class A uniform to check fishermen, it was said that I was "showing the flag." In that way, I would check the obvious shore fisherman for his current fishing license and limit of fish.

Sportsmen would inform me that I should get to the creek by 7:00 am; that is when fishermen will be snagging salmon. When I appeared in my Class A uniform I could feel all those eyes on me. I knew what they were thinking. *I hope he don't come over here."*

After three or four years as a conservation officer, I could put fishermen into categories. There were three common excuses. I would scan the area closest to me and notice a likely candidate: fishing pole, no boots, wearing sneakers, no gloves, no hat. He was the one I would check first. Most times I was right.

"Sir, check your fishing license. Sir, yes you. Check your fishing license."

"Oh, I left it home."

Then I would give him the old twenty questions: how much did it cost, where did you get it, what color is it? By then I knew it was time for a trip to the car.

Often while checking a group of fishermen I would notice one that saw me and would drop his pole like it was on fire. This was a sure bet.

"Sir, check your fishing license please."

"Oh, I wasn't fishing."

"Well, you had this pole in your hand with the line in the water…you were fishing."

Another common excuse was,

"I don't have a license. I was just trying it out to see if I like it."

Back at the car it was time to finish with the paper work and head patrol car 7N913 back to headquarters for supper.

Another successful day.

It was the best experience I could have had. I wanted to be a Forest Range since I was a child. I served 37 years as a Conservation Officer. Would not want another profession.

Jerry Sporer, Retired Lt. ECO.

A Spring Night

It was a beautiful spring night, the kind that any conservation officer would appreciate. The temperature was about 40 degrees, the air was still, and the spring peepers were in fine form. I love to hear their music. I felt that all was well in my little corner of the world.

At 9:15 PM, I told my wife that I was headed out to check the streams for any illegal spearing. Spearing was considered to be a rite of spring for the locals. They would dig out their kerosene lanterns, hip boots and spears from winter storage and head out to spear some suckers.

Twenty minutes later I was driving down Hess Road, approaching Lake Road. I made a left turn onto Lake Road and within 100 yards stopped at Keg Creek. In the spring this creek would support trout, suckers, northern pike, or smelt, depending on the night.

It was a beautiful night and I couldn't believe I saw only one car parked. I pulled my marked state car into a hidden driveway and proceeded to put on my hip boots and a cover jacket over my state coat. I could see a flashlight bouncing around inside the five-foot culvert that went under the state highway. A second person stood on top of the culvert and, when I reached the edge of the road, I could tell it was a young lady, probably in her early twenties. I did not identify myself, but asked how the fishing was. Her first words to me were,

"SSShhh. Be quiet. The game warden might hear us."

I was thinking that this could be very interesting. I looked in the culvert and saw a big young man with a dip net in his hand. He made a swing with the net and came up with a big rainbow trout. Taking the trout out of the net, he threw it up on the bank. I said to the young lady,

"Nice fish."

She replied, "I told you to be quiet, the game warden might hear us."

I still couldn't believe this was happening. The guy in the culvert came out with another fish in the net. He looked up at me and said hello and I said,

"Dick Lang, Conservation Officer. Let's get the other trout you threw up on the bank, then come over to my car."

I gave him a ticket and never saw him again for 35 years. Then, at his father's funeral, we made eye contact and I knew what was going through his mind. In a whisper I leaned over to him and asked,

"Did you marry that girl?"

"No," he said, and then started to laugh.

Funny Statements

You would not believe how polite the sporting public can be. I found that out over the many times I wrote a ticket, usually for fishing without a license. The individual receiving the ticket would often say "Thank you." And this did not just happen once or twice, it was common. I would say to myself "What nice manners he has." Or, maybe he just could not think of anything else to say, so he said "Thank you."

Another interesting comment made to me by the public was "How's business?" Well, there are two ways one can take that statement. If I was in the private sector that statement would mean, "Is your business doing well?" But, in my world as an environmental conservation police officer, I think the public was usually referring to how many tickets I wrote for the state that day. I would usually come back with the statement, "Business is out there."

Numerous times over my 34-year career the non-hunting public asked me why I carried a gun. I would explain to them that, first of all, we are police officers and were required to wear sidearms. Secondly, we meet more people with firearms than any other police agency, and conservation officers throughout the United States are assaulted more than any other police department. We must be prepared and proficient in the use of our firearm. Some of the public must think we just go about hugging trees and catching and releasing little rabbits. Not so!

When answering the telephone I never knew how the conversation was going to begin. "Hello is the *conversation* officer there?" I knew I had the gift of gab, but I didn't think I was the conversation officer!

Other phone greetings included, "Is the gamie there? Is the warden there? Is the game warden there?"

I would gently correct them and say, "This is Dick Lang, Conservation Officer." I always knew they meant me. I just wonder what they called me behind my back. I am sure they were always statements that showed respect?! Ha Ha.

Night Fishing is Always Exciting

It was 6:30 PM on a Saturday in late October and I had just radioed Environmental Conservation Officer Jim Rogers to ask for his assistance.

"Jim, there are two cars at Keg Creek and I would like your help with a check."

Jim replied, "Sure, Dick. I'm in Wilson, I'll see you in about twenty minutes."

Jim arrived and parked in a secluded drive among an apple orchard the farmer had given us permission to use. I said, "Let's go upstream to that light."

As we closed in on the light, we could see there were two fishermen with lanterns. Approaching from behind we could see they were attempting to catch rainbow trout. They were having a great time. There was only one thing wrong, they were snagging the trout. Since the creek was so narrow, it was easy to snag them. Three trout were tossed within a few feet of our location. What a time they were having! After they snagged a trout they would high-five each other and say such things as,

"Can't wait to show these fish to Dad. Dad is going to s--- when he sees all these fish."

After watching them for twenty minutes, we decided it was time to make our presence known. They were startled as we turned our lights on and identified ourselves.

"Guys, let's check your fishing licenses. Licenses are fine, but we do have a problem and you know what it is, snagging fish, and you each have one fish over the limit. I'm sorry to say, but Dad is going to s--- when he sees all these tickets."

Things That Happened Only Once

Often while doing my job, a thought would pop into my head and I would wonder how I would handle a certain situation if it happened to me. Maybe I would be driving through the swamp and wonder why I'd never caught someone stealing one of those evergreen trees. Or, I would be paging through the syllabus and would see in bold letters: frog season. I had yet to catch someone taking frogs out of season. It was getting late in my career and I didn't know if I would get the chance to experience everything I wanted to, but here are a few of my stories.

It was December 18, 1984 and I was on the Owens Bartell Road patrolling the Tonawanda Wildlife Area (better known as the swamp) for rabbit hunters or any other strange thing that might happen in front of me. It was 11:30 AM and the sun was just starting to melt the ice on the road when I saw a vehicle by the side of the road with the trunk up and two guys standing next to it. Exiting my patrol car, my mind started turning and I thought, *This is my lucky day.* There in the trunk was a fresh-cut evergreen tree that I could tell had been dragged through the snow from the swamp.

I turned to the two young men and said,

"Gentlemen, this is not the meaning of Christmas, to steal a Christmas tree."

They hung their heads and did not have a lot to say.

"Boys, give me your driver's licenses."

They handed me their licenses and I proceeded back to my patrol car to look up the section of law pertaining to the removal of trees off state property. In a few minutes I came back with the two tickets returnable at the local court. I removed the tree from their trunk and placed it in my vehicle. In my years as an officer I had come to know who needed clothes, food or a Christmas tree and I had just the family for that tree.

***

It was a hot August 23, 1978 when I received a call from a resident of the City of Lockport. It was 1:00 PM and I had stopped at my home for lunch and to answer any complaints I may have received. There weren't any complaints but the telephone was ringing as I entered the kitchen. The caller on the other end of the line was very agitated.

"Hello. My neighbor just shot an owl."

"Where did this take place?"

"On East Avenue in the city of Lockport."

I got the address and was in a hurry to get there before the owl was disposed of. I thought there must be something more to this story. Why would someone shot an owl in the city? Within ten minutes I was pulling into the driveway of the person in question. There, sitting on the porch, was an elderly male in a cut-off tee shirt, with a .22 rifle across his lap.

"Hi, what's going on?"

"I had to shoot that owl, and there are more of them I am going to get."

"Sir, lets talk this over."

I stretched my arm out while asking for the rifle. He placed it my hand. Sitting down next to him I began to ask questions.

"Why are you mad at this little Screech Owl?"

"These dam owls are keeping me up all night long. I can't sleep with all the noise they're making."

"But you cannot discharge a firearm in the city and the owl is a protected bird."

Then I asked the big question.

"Sir, how old are you?"

"Eighty Four."

I thought to myself, *Eighty four. Now what am I going to do?* I got this on a complaint. I don't condone this, but it's going to look like I'm picking on old people. On the other hand, I felt this was much too severe for just a warning. Returning to my car with the .22 rifle I wrote two tickets, one for discharging a firearm within 500 feet of a dwelling and the other for taking a protected bird, the Screech Owl.

***

I had always told myself I would not retire until I wrote a ticket for taking frogs out of season. Well, I may have said it, but deep down I knew there was a good chance that I might retire first and may not ever get a frog violation.

On April 18, 2001 I was just leaving the Town of Newfane Town Hall when the Niagara County

Sheriff's radio called ENCON 7N913, my car number.

"7N913 would you contact Zone 6. They have a complaint of discharging a firearm along the railroad tracks off Charlottesville Road, Town of Newfane."

This could be my lucky day. In less than five minutes I pulled in behind the sheriff's patrol car where the two possible violators were in tow with the deputy sheriff.

"Hi," I said, "What's going on?"

"Oh these three guys were shooting frogs off the railroad tracks."

"Did you get any?"

"Oh yea, we got a few," the guy in the blue shirt said as he handed me a bag with ten frogs in it.

"Gentlemen do you know when frog season begins?"

"I thought it was open now."

"No, it does not open until June 15th and it closes September 30th."

"Oh boy, I think we're in trouble."

"Why don't you guys sit right here while I go back to my car."

I thanked the deputy and wrote out three tickets for taking frogs out of season. I was laughing to myself as I handed them the tickets. Thanks guys for making my day.

Region 9 Officers Block Meeting
Dick is in the middle of the back row.

Addicted to Fishing

In my thirty-four years as a conservation officer, I made lots of arrests but, for me and a handful of officers from the Buffalo Region, there was only one that stood head and shoulders above the other violators. His name was Bart Sanderson, from Tonawanda, New York. I was the first to come in contact with this young man. In the beginning he was just another fish and game violator, but he gained notoriety as his name continued to show up in Western New York courts. He progressed from killing game to killing a young female jogger in Wisconsin, and is now serving a life sentence for second-degree murder.

It was September 9, 1985 and it was a beautiful day. The sun was bright, there was a bite in the air, and I had a feeling there would be some snagging going on at the power plant. The power plant was located in the town of Lewiston, in the lower Niagara River, and was a hot spot for the spawning run of King salmon, Coho salmon, and brown and steelhead trout. There hadn't been fish this size in the Niagara River since the sturgeon. It was a huge success story for the fishermen and the State of New York, a win-win situation. It was a great economic bonanza and there were thousands of large fish; what more could we ask for. But, after five years of allowing snagging in the waters off Lake Ontario, our Fisheries Department had decided it was not ethical and should be phased out. But, they couldn't phase out the desire to snag fish illegally. The water temperature was falling into the lower fifties and upper forties and fishing fever had taken over. Hundreds of people would converge on the area around the power plant just to catch those thirty-pound King salmon.

I had decided to park my car inside the gate where the fishermen could not see my marked law-enforcement auto. The gate slid open as the guard saw me approaching and allowed me to enter a restricted area. Getting out of my car I put on the hunting jacket I used to cover my uniform shirt. I was also wearing a camo hat and green pants without a stripe. I was as camouflaged as I could get. I also had a small pad and pen to write down descriptions of the many varieties of fishermen.

The bank all around the power plant was covered with huge rocks. As I exited the plant I decided to turn right and watch a group of fishermen. I counted fifteen in the group and zeroed in on a young man, brown-haired, about 5'10" with a pencil-thin mustache. He went down to the river and started ripping at the water with a sideways motion, gripping a large three-pronged hook we called a snag hook. He kept glancing around to see if he was the only one snagging. At that time he was. Rip, he continued to make that motion. He was very serious. Bang, he got one. Reeling a huge salmon up on the rocks, he proceeded to drag it up to an older man who took up the position of protector of the fish. After twenty minutes watching this guy snag three salmon I identified myself and told them he was in violation of snagging fish, which is prohibited. The older gentleman explained that he was in bad health and would appreciate it if I could give his son a break this time. I explained that I felt this was intentional and that he was going to get a ticket for snagging fish. I then gave the defendant a ticket, and told him I would see him in Lewiston Court in two weeks. Two weeks went by and Conservation Officer Neil Ross and I had our share of fishing cases but Mr. Sanderson's stood out from the rest. In court on the appointed day, Officer Ross and I approached the bench. Sanderson was asked if he pleaded guilty or not guilty.

"Guilty, but your Honor, I have no money at this time."

Judge Lombardi said in a stern voice,

"That will be $150 and you have two weeks to pay it."

Sanderson said nothing. He signed the necessary paperwork and left the court.

Neil and I stopped to get a coffee in town and then headed down to the river to check a few fishermen. After an hour, I followed Officer Ross to the power plant where we saw ten vehicles parked. I said,

"Let's go, Neil. I think we can do some business tonight."

Quietly exiting our vehicles I motioned to Neil and pointed out the fishermen. We stood back and watched who was fishing and who was snagging those thirty-pound salmon. Turning my light on the first guy I saw, I couldn't believe my eyes. It was Bart Sanderson!

"Bart, the judge told you he never wanted to see you in court for this violation again and here you are snagging fish a little over a hour after you left court."

"Well, I don't have any money so I came here to catch fish and sell them to make the fine money."

I proceeded to take him up to my patrol car and wrote him another ticket for the same violation - snagging trout.

Three years went by and I didn't see him in my area, but he was showing up in Chautauqua, Erie and Niagara Counties. The guy got around! He was apprehended in September of 1986 by Officer Matt Pestinger for fishing without a license and for snagging fish. I remembered what Judge Haseley of Lewiston had said in October of 1985,

"Mr. Sanderson, I don't ever want to see you in this court again or you will be going to jail."

Well, this time the same judge sent him to jail for 10 days and added a $250 fine. Environmental Conservation Officer Neil Ross was the next arresting officer on March 23, 1987. Fishing without a license again. Then he left the immediate area and went to Chautauqua County where Officer Don Malmrose wrote him up for failure to carry his fishing license. Don had no way of knowing the guy's license was already revoked. On May 17, 1988, Officer Jim Rogers apprehended him on Grand Island for fishing while revoked. Then it was back to Chautauqua County where Officer Malmrose apprehended him for fishing while revoked. Up to this time he always paid his fines; most of them were at the maximum of $250. But now he jumped over another line and started to hunt deer during daylight hours. He would hunt with either a gun or a bow, and this time it was Officer Neil Ross who found him deer hunting in open area between a housing development and New York State Route 290. Of course he did not have a big game license and he was also in violation of hunting next to the interstate, in a no-hunting area. The Town of Amherst Police had Sanderson in tow by the time Conservation Officer Ross met them at the town hall. Ross then issued Sanderson tickets for hunting without a license, not having an archery stamp, and hunting deer in a closed area.

On October 23, 1988, the salmon were once again in 18-Mile Creek, in the Town of Newfane, and everyone was fish happy. No one who fished the streams off Lake Ontario had ever seen salmon this big. It was 3:00 PM and I had the thought that tonight would be a good night to give those salmon some protection. New York State had just changed the fishing regulations to extend from a half-hour before sunup to a half-hour after sundown. But, to some, it was just too much of a temptation to snag a fish at night when no one else was in the stream.

As I approached the Burt Dam, I saw three cars, an old pickup truck, and a blue Dodge van. I parked my marked patrol car behind an apple cold-storage building where it would be hidden. I threw on my cover coat and camo hat and grabbed a good flashlight that I wouldn't turn on until I needed to. I had been down this bank hundreds of times in the dark, so I should not need my flashlight. But, I still needed some things that I couldn't wear on my gun belt...confidence, moxie, and the belief that I could handle whatever came my way.

My ears strained to hear any unusual sound that might be salmon making their way to the dam, or a fisherman slowly moving through the water. Then I heard a familiar clunk, the sound of a weighted, 3-barbed hook with a lead weight attached. I would know that sound anywhere. Having reached the creek I saw two silhouettes moving slowly in the shallows. I took my 7x35 binoculars from beneath my coat. Yea, they were snagging. Should I move in now or watch a while to see if they snag one? After a few minutes, I decided, *That's enough, they can't seem to get one. Let's surprise them.*

"Hi guys. Dick Lang, Conservation Officer, checking fishing licenses."

They gave me that blank look that tells me - what, are you crazy? I don't have a license. Only one of them had any identification, so after a few moments we headed up the path to my car. In the dark I didn't recognize either of them. The one kid showed me his driver's license, but the other one didn't have one.

I took the second guy about twenty yards from the car and asked his name. He told me he was Clarence Williams. We went back to the car and I did the same thing with the first guy, who agreed...that's Clarence Williams. So I wrote a couple of tickets for each man for snagging, fishing without a license, and fishing after hours. The court date came and went and no one showed up. Now I was mad. I hate guys who ignore my tickets. I called the phone number for Clarence Williams. Bad number. Now I was really mad. I called the other guy who had been with him.

"Ricky, let's get one thing straight. If I don't get his correct name, you are getting some more tickets, do you understand?"

"Yes, Mr. Lang."

"Well, who is it?"

"Bart Sanderson."

Why, that SOB.

"Ricky, I am going to have you sign a statement saying who that was."

"Okay, no problem."

Fast forward to the spring of 1990 when I called Environmental Conservation Officer Jim Rogers.

"Jim, I found out where Sanderson works. I would appreciate it if you could go with me to execute an arrest warrant on him."

"Sure, let's do it Thursday, the 14th."

Ricky had told me Sanderson was working at a lumberyard in Buffalo. Arriving at the lumberyard we proceeded to the office, where we identified ourselves, explaining we were there to serve an arrest warrant on one of their employees, Bart Sanderson. The foreman proceeded to tell me what a good worker he was.

"That's a surprise," I said. "No one I have talked to has much good to say about him."

Then, a few breaths later, he says,

"That's it. He's fired."

Wow. One minute he's a good worker and the next minute he's fired. We walked over to Sanderson, telling him he was under arrest. I handcuffed him and placed him in the back seat of my car. Officer Rogers read him his rights. I had already made arrangements for one of my Newfane Judges to meet us at the town hall. In less than a hour we were there and I took Sanderson by the arm and brought him before Judge Joseph Slomba. After reading the charges the judge asked Sanderson how he wanted to plead.

"Guilty your Honor, on both charges."

"Before I pronounce sentence, do you have anything to say?"

"Yes, your Honor, I need help. I am addicted to fishing. I need help."

"Well, the best we can do is the Niagara County Jail for 30 days and a $500 fine. Officers, here are the commitment papers."

Within twenty minutes he was at the Niagara County Hilton (jail). Addicted to fishing?! That was a new one. I was going to have to remember that one.

Dick, with salmon and spears

Don't Shoot

It was opening day of the 1987 duck season at the Tonawanda Wildlife Area and I was meeting Environmental Conservation Officers Harold Keppner and Neil Ross in the parking lot at 5:30 AM.

It was about 36 degrees, crisp and clear, with lots of stars. We each put on our hunting gear, hip boots, an old canvas coat over our uniform shirt, and I picked up my double barrel shotgun. I said to Harry,

"Maybe this will be our lucky day."

What I meant by that was, maybe, finally, we might get the hunters that always start the swamp shooting early. The season started at one half hour before sunup and I could never understand why duck hunters wanted to start twenty minutes before legal shooting time. You couldn't see your hand in front of your face, let alone a duck.

We decided to use the maintenance road going back to the dike. Closing our car doors quietly, we proceeded down the trail. There were hunters everywhere, hundreds of them. I wondered, *When will the first shot go off?* Walking single file, we were almost stepping on one another when I saw a group of five hunters within six feet of us. You could tell by their motions that they wanted to shot.

Officer Ross and I were ready. Was this the group that was going to start the shooting early? Officer Keppner felt that he must be a good sportsman and he told them,

"Don't shoot."

But they ignored him. He told them again,

"Don't shoot."

I knew this group was geared up and were going to shoot no matter what. I saw the silhouette of what looked like ten Mallard ducks proceeding within range of our group of duck hunters. Will the temptation be too much? All of a sudden, the one closest to Officer Keppner fired his 12-gauge, Bang, Bang, setting off the whole swamp. Harry yelled,

"I told you not to shoot. Now you're under arrest."

I could not believe it. After all these years, I was finally standing right next to the guys who started the early shooting. They were seventeen minutes early. We rounded up all five, requested their hunting licenses with a waterfowl stamp, issued each of them citations for hunting before legal shooting hours and left feeling very good, knowing that we had finally got the group that started the early shooting.

Exotic Wildlife

I've had my share of unusual wildlife cases, but 1990 was the year of three especially strange critter cases.

In February, I received a complaint that a lynx cat was being held as a pet in the town of Pendleton. The owner of the cat had a reputation of being a person who would cross the line if the opportunity presented itself.

At this time, law enforcement had an environmental conservation officer assigned to work as a specialist in the endangered species field. That officer was Dan Sullivan, whom I enjoyed working with. He was about 10 years younger than I was, but we sure clicked when we worked together. I called Dan the night before, setting up a time and date to go see if this complaint was for real.

Milt Messing possessed the cat and also owned a car repair shop. The shop just happened to be in the direction I was headed to meet Dan, so I checked it out as I went by. Sure enough, he was there. I met Officer Sullivan at the Lockport Town Hall, we shared information, he jumped in my vehicle and we headed for the Messing home on Main Street in Pendleton.

We pulled in the driveway, walked up to the door and knocked, but no one answered. Time went by, and still no answer. We went to look in the windows to see if we could see anything and just then, we heard the door start to open. Regaining our composure, we noticed a young girl in her late teens at the door.

"Hi, would Mr. Messing be home?"

"No, he's at work."

"I understand you have a lynx cat?"

"Oh yes we have one."

"Could we see it?"

"Sure."

Dan and I looked at each other. This was going to be easy. She yelled, "Kitty" and, with that, a full-grown lynx ran around the corner and stood next to her. The next thing we know, the cat jumped up into her arms. We could not believe our eyes. Now the cat was purring like a house cat.

"Where did he get the cat?"

"Out of one of those trapping magazines."

"How long has he had it?"

"Three years."

I can't believe he's had it three years and I never heard about it until now.

"What do you feed it?"

"Chicken. Come on in I'll show you where we raise them."

We followed her to the basement where we saw about twenty half-grown chickens inside a fence. No wonder the cat looked so healthy.

"Do you know you cannot possess this animal?"

"Oh, I thought he had a permit."

"No, he doesn't"

We decided to give her a receipt for the animal and be off. We asked her to please put the cat in our carrying cage since he was comfortable with her. With the lynx secured in the cage, we went off to the shop to hear Milt Messing's reason for keeping the lynx. As we exited our green sedan, a slim, tall guy stood up.

"Hi Milt, Dick Lang, Conservation Officer."

"Yea, I hear you were looking for me."

"We got your lynx cat."

"You do? Well, I was going to get a permit, but before I knew it, three years had passed."

"Well, you're too late. You cannot possess this cat. Milt, the cat will be going to the Buffalo Zoo, and you will be getting a ticket to appear in local court."

The Buffalo Zoo now had another lynx and the state had collected a $250 fine.

***

Monday night, April 21st, I was just finishing supper when the phone rang.

"Hi Dick. I don't want to tell you who this is, but Chester Avery has a wolf chained up behind his house."

"Is that the Avery that lives in Lowertown?"

"Sure is. He has a couple of Dobermans next to the wolf."

"Are you sure it's a wolf?"

"Trust me, it's a wolf. Go check it out."

"Thanks, I will."

I hung up the phone and called Endangered Species Officer Dan Sullivan.

"Dan, I need you for another strange wild animal case."

"What is it this time?"

"A wolf."

"What is going on in Niagara County?"

"I don't know, maybe it's something in the water. Can you meet me tomorrow at 8:00AM?"

Dan arrived at my home, loaded his equipment in my car, and we were off for Lockport. It was a damp, cool day, around 45 degrees. When we arrived at the Avery's and drove up the long driveway, I could see three doghouses with different critters in them. Dan and I went to the door and rang the bell. I could hear it ringing inside, but no one was answering. Now three of those nasty dogs started barking at us. Except the animal in the middle was definitely not a dog. It did not bark at us like the other two. It just kept moving very slowly back in forth in front of the doghouse looking at us with those beady eyes, like it wanted to make lunch out of us. The wolf had a heavy chain around its neck attached to his wolf house (it used to be called a doghouse) with his name written above the entrance. I discovered his name was Devil (Fitting!). Okay, we knew his name, but I wasn't getting too close to Devil.

"Dan, let's go down to Chester's shop and see what answers he gives us."

Chester had a motorcycle shop just north of town. I was sure that, as we pulled into the parking lot with a marked State Conservation Car, Chester knew who we were. Chester was another one of those with a dubious reputation.

"Conservation Officers Dick Lang and Dan Sullivan. We're here to see if you have a permit for that wolf at your home on West Street."

"No, I don't have a permit."

Of course, we already knew that. I had already checked that out with Special Licenses in Albany, but I still had to ask.

"Why did you want to get a wolf?"

"I like wolves. He won't hurt anyone."

Dan asked for his driver's license and proceeded to write a ticket for the Town of Lockport Court.

"Chester we don't have a cage with us but we will be back tomorrow to take him."

"Why do you have to seize him?"

"I told you once, he is a dangerous, wild, illegal animal, and you need a New York State permit for him."

Dan gave him the ticket and away we went.

Wednesday morning Dan arrived in a truck with a big box cage on it. We headed out to Chester's.

"What are the odds? I'll bet he's gone."

"I'll bet you're right."

As we pulled up the driveway, all we could see was a chain lying on the ground without a wolf attached.

"Okay, let's go to the shop again and see what answer we get this time."

"Chester, what did you do with the wolf?"

"A friend of mine took him to Canada."

"Who is that?"

"I don't know his name."

Well for what it's worth, at least we didn't have to transport him. All the time I was figuring that wolf would show up some place. I'll bet he didn't go too far.

Fast forward to November of 1993. I got a call from Conservation Officer Jeff Rupp, of Cattaraugus County.

"Dick, I have to tell you about this wolf that came from Niagara County."

"I think I know the wolf you are talking about. Is its name Devil?"

"Yes, it is."

I called Bob, the local veterinarian, to assist me with a cage. He brought the cage and offered to house the animal until we decided what to do with it. He put it in a shed next to his barn and during the night he heard all this loud noise. It sounded terrible. He jumped out of bed, grabbed his rifle and light, and ran outside to find the wolf making a huge hole in the side of the shed. It was like he had gone insane. He was ripping the wood apart from the inside with his teeth. Well, Bob couldn't take any chances, so before the wolf exited the shed completely, he killed it with a bullet from his rifle. I was relieved that the animal did not escape and create havoc all over Cattaraugus County.

***

It was now June and school was about to close for the summer, but not before I would have one more exotic animal case. Again I got specialist Dan Sullivan to assist.

"Dan, you won't believe it, but there's a live alligator in an aquarium at the bus garage. Meet me at my place at 8:00 tomorrow morning. Oh, and bring a cage."

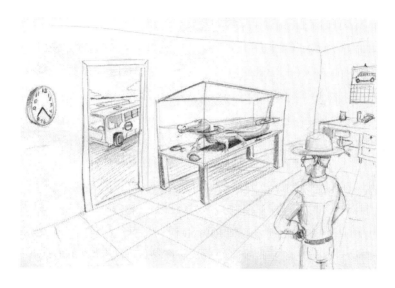

Dan always enjoyed working with me because I always came up with the most unusual cases. Dan and I drove to the bus garage and knocked on the door. A voice from inside welcomed us in. I open the door and, stepping inside, said,

"Hi, is Jim here?"

"How can I help you?"

"I understand you have an alligator in your office?"

"Yes, I do. Come in and take a look."

Sure enough. There was a three-foot alligator in a two-and-a-half foot aquarium. His tail was curled up, he had no room to move and he looked awfully uncomfortable.

"Jim, how long have you had this critter?"

"Two years."

"Where did you get it?"

"Oh, I bought it from a pet shop in Maryland when it was about 6 inches long."

"Do you have a permit?"

"Well, I was going to get one."

"I'm afraid that's not the right answer. Jim, we are going to seize the alligator and take it to the Buffalo Zoo."

Dan wrote the ticket for possessing an endangered species without a permit.

What a year for strange animals. They sure made things interesting.

Golf Course Deer

After being on the job for fifteen years, all I had to
have was an inch and I would work very hard to get
the mile. It was Sunday morning, November 15,
1986, and I was relaxing, reading the Sunday
morning paper when the telephone rang.

"Dick, I don't want to give you my name, but my
brother shot a deer last night off the golf course."

I don't have any patience with that stuff, it really
bothers me.

"Which golf course?'

"The one off Lake Avenue in the Town of Lockport."

"The one on the left going north?"

"Yea, that's the one."

"Where is the deer?"

"It's in the freezer at his house."

"So, who were all the people involved."

"Kyle Chambers and Elliot Martin."

"What car was he driving?"

"That big old brown Dodge that sits next to the house."

Oh, I knew them all right. I had caught them snagging salmon down near the Burt Dam without a license. They had paid for that mistake; now let's see how this one goes. I loved these kinds of investigations. They gave me half a loaf, now let's see if I can get it all.

I ran upstairs, put on my full dress uniform and buckled up my .357. I gave my sweetie a kiss and a smile and said,

"See you in a couple of hours."

Conservation officers wives are used to their husbands running off at all hours and all days of the

253

week. Hurrying out the front door, I started planning my investigation. I had a general idea where the suspect's home was located. I found it without any trouble and also spotted the auto, the old brown Dodge that the complainant had used for his deerjacking. I quickly checked the bumper as I headed towards the door and saw the blood and deer hair on the trunk and bumper. I was excited and confident. I would get my man.

I knocked on the door and heard footsteps approaching. Moments later the door opened and Kyle stood there. His hair was a mess and he had a nasty growth of beard.

"Hi Kyle. I received a complaint that you and Elliot were at the golf course taking a deer at 2:25 AM. Get your shoes on and let's check the truck on the Dodge."

Kyle made some muffled sounds and struggled with his shoes.

Being a little sarcastic, I said,

"Kyle, look at that deer hair and blood. Let's see what's in the trunk."

Swinging up the trunk we stared into an empty trunk. Well, not quite empty. There was a lot of blood and hair but no deer.

"Okay Kyle, I want the deer meat NOW. All I need for a conviction is deer hair and blood so you're getting a ticket no matter what."

He decided not to argue with me and we headed back to the house. He opened the freezer door over the refrigerator and I saw many packs of what I considered to be deer meat. I counted the packages and gave him a receipt and a ticket for the town of Lockport Court. I also got a statement from Kyle incriminating Elliot Martin as his partner in the golf course deer caper.

As I drove home I was satisfied, but dumbfounded that Kyle, who has had many encounters with the local police, rolled over so easily. Maybe he felt I knew too much. As the saying goes among game wardens, it seems the harder you look the harder it is to find a violation. Then there are the times when they just fall in your lap. As my partner, Kimpton Vosburg, used to say, "Even a blind pig gets an acorn once in awhile."

Albany DEC Convention, 2000
Dick is in 2nd last row, 2nd from left.

The Judges

I had such great judges, all "salt of the earth" types.
None of them were lawyers. They were farmers,
small businessmen, teachers, or they worked for a
large corporation. Their law degree came from good
solid common sense. They had names like Buster,
George, Beryl, Wes, John, Joe, Will, Hack, Clive
and, of course, Midge. They were all down-to-earth
people who knew the law and were always available
and accommodating. Many of them had an office in
their own home to arraign or settle cases. Instead of
taking defendants to town hall, you would take them
to the judge's home, sometimes to the kitchen table,
sometimes to a room set aside strictly for that
purpose.

In my first twelve years as a conservation officer, I
had a judge with many years experience behind him,

George Gallagher. What a great guy. George was a tall, thin man with wispy gray hair and a deep, drawn-out voice. You could not help but like him. He was a retired farmer with an office in his basement. All the police officers in the area used George for arraignments. You never used George before three in the afternoon but, after that, he was available all night long. There were many times I would call him to tell him I would be working late checking duck hunters and, if I had a violation, I knew I could take him right over.

Upon our arrival, George would escort us through the basement to his office. A large American flag hung behind his desk. He would ask me, "What do we have officer?" I would read the charge and he would ask how the violator wanted to plead. Most of the time it was guilty. The fine would be set, the defendant would pay, then be free to leave. At that time the judge did not have a court clerk. He would smile, look at me, slide a huge book called a docket my way and tell me, "Fill it out." So, I would put in all the necessary information, the name, address, charge and fine, then close the docket.

Then there was Will. Will was great for morning appearances. He lived in the Town of Newfane where a huge fishing activity was taking place. On numerous occasions, I would catch large numbers of people fishing without a license, snagging trout, and numerous other violations late in the day. I would set aside a designated meeting place and time and then all the defendants would follow me to the judge's office.

On one occasion, I had witnessed two individuals snagging salmon in 18-Mile Creek. They seemed like okay guys and I found out more about them as I was writing their tickets. They were from New York City and had flown to Buffalo, rented a car and come to Newfane to do some salmon fishing. The next morning they were at the designated spot and we proceeded to the judge's office. The judge took a moment to read the charges, then asked the defendants how they pled. "Guilty, your Honor." They reached for their wallets and removed the necessary fine money. Then, one of them spoke up.

"Judge, could I ask a favor of you?"

"What's that?" Will asked.

"We would like to have our picture taken with you while we are holding our tickets so we can show our buddies back in New York City."

Everyone smiled as I took the pictures. Then it was my turn to be in the photo to show the boys back home. It sure made for a memorable story.

It seems that many of my judges stick in my mind as some of the most interesting people I have met. The last judge I will give special attention to is Beryl Coleman. Beryl came from Somerset, a very rural town where crime was second nature to many. The conservation violators in town were also the burglars and the muggers. It was a family tradition. If grandfather was a poacher, his son picked it up and then taught the grandson as the grandfather was retiring. Judge Coleman was very pro law enforcement and ruled his court with an iron hand, although he could be compassionate when needed. Beryl set the state record for serving fifty years as a town justice and was the right judge at the right time.

One case that comes to mind was an illegal salmon case at 18-Mile Creek, in Burt. Burt was not in the town of Somerset but we ended up at Judge

Coleman's court because the Newfane judges were unavailable. It was late October and I had contacted Environmental Conservation Officer Matt Pestinger to see if he wanted to go out and check for late snaggers at the Burt Dam. We both agreed that this felt like the right night to go. By 10:30 PM we had parked our cars and were proceeding quietly along the bank of the creek. It was a great experience to see the sky lit up with so many stars and no hint of wind. It was deadly quiet with just the noise of the salmon cutting through the water and the sound of the water flowing over the dam.

We got within fifty yards of the dam before we could see light from the lanterns flickering off the water. We took up positions in an old, abandoned, stone building. I was surprised at how much I was able to see with my 7x35 binoculars. The light from the lanterns showed me there were two men on the west side of the creek and seven on our side, less than twenty yards from our location. They were speaking Spanish. I tapped Officer Pestinger lightly, whispering, "I know these guys." They were from Buffalo. I had told them that if I ever caught them down here again I would take them all to jail. The last time I caught them I had to get arrest warrants to pick them up and it took months to round them all up. "Okay," said Pestinger, "let's go check them out."

We started with the ones on our side of the creek. None of the seven had a fishing license and all were snagging. I could tell the two on the other side of the creek were getting nervous. I left the seven on the east side with Pestinger and sprinted across the creek to grab those two. They were climbing the bank as I screamed, "STOP. Conservation Officer Lang." I got close enough to grab one by the ankle. I held on hard enough to pull him down and arrest him, but the second one got away. He must have walked all the way back to Buffalo because we never found him.

I met Officer Pestinger and we marched the eight men to our patrol cars. We were in the process of writing tickets when a Deputy Sheriff from the Niagara County Sheriff's Department appeared. To speed things up, the deputy was gracious enough to help us with our tickets. It was now 1:30 AM and no judges were available in the Town of Newfane. We contacted Judge Beryl Coleman, of Somerset, who said to bring them right over.

After a brief meeting with the judge, the tickets and charges were explained to the defendants and all pled guilty. The judge set $150 fine for each charge. None were able to pay. We left the Somerset Court for the Niagara County Jail, where they spent a combination of fine and days served. I never saw them again.

A Time and Place for a Uniform

After 34 years it was still neat to get out of bed in the morning and decide I was wearing my Class A uniform that day. The Class A was the dress uniform with a stripe down the pants, sharp creases, the uniform coat with patches and the Stetson hat, as clean as if it had just come out of the box. My decision on how to dress depended on what I was doing that day. After you had been an environmental conservation officer for many years, you knew when to wear the right equipment.

Many days in the month of October I would drive to 18-Mile Creek to check salmon and trout fishermen. I would not only be checking their current fishing license, I would also check to see if they were over their limit, or check for the dreaded snagging of fish.

As I approached the Burt Dam parking lot, I picked up the microphone and checked in with the office.

"7N913 to Buffalo. I will be out of service at the Burt Dam."

I checked the back seat of my patrol car to be sure I had a variety of clothes with me, just in case I had to play Superman and change back into my Class C uniform. There were a couple hundred fishermen from all over New York State, and many other states like Ohio, Pennsylvania, and West Virginia. I enjoyed the conversations I had with these guys. They are great fishermen, just as long as you keep in the back of your mind that they are determined to go home with a salmon, no matter what.

I removed my badge from my shirt pocket and placed it in a pocket in my uniform jacket where I could remove it quickly. I approached the first guy in the water and used my million-dollar line,

"Conservation Officer Lang, checking your fishing license please."

Many had it handy and quickly gave it to me. While I was waiting for this one to find his license I was scanning the fishermen in the direction I was headed, watching to see who was going to drop their pole like it was on fire and then walk around ignoring it like they didn't know where it came from.

The fisherman in front of me handed me his license. I verified the date and color and returned it with a thank you. Then I approached the second man,

"Hi, Dick Lang, Conservation Officer, check your fishing license please."

"Oh I wasn't fishing, I was just seeing if I would like it."

I wish I had a dollar for every time I heard that excuse. Once you had the pole in your hand, you were fishing. And you got a ticket.

It was a beautiful October day with hundreds of salmon fishermen in 18-Mile Creek. Boy, was I lucky to have this fishing opportunity in my area. Driving up Route 18, I made a left into Fisherman's Park and saw hundreds of vehicles, campers, pickups, and cars, with license plates from all over the United States. This was so good for our local economy. The restaurants, motels and campgrounds were full of the out-of-staters, as we called them. The attendant opened the door to the guard shack.

"Hi Jim, how are the fish running?" I asked.

"We're seeing a lot of salmon and a few browns. Looks like a good day for a check."

I looked for a place to park my marked patrol car where it would not stand out and reported to the office.

"7N913 to Buffalo. I will be out of service in Newfane."

"Buffalo received."

I could have said "out of service at Burt Dam" but I never liked to be too specific because so many folks have police scanners and I wanted to give myself the best possible edge.

Getting out of the car, I opened the back door and pulled out my cover jacket. This jacket had been with me throughout my entire career. It was an old canvas hunting coat, a size bigger than my normal jacket. I added my camo army cap and my 16" rubber boots and I was ready to hit the creek. On my way I passed many a successful fisherman dragging a large salmon or two up the hill to their vehicle. Most of them had a smile on their face so I was pretty sure they'd had a good time. All I wanted from these visitors was to play by the rules, spend some money and go home safely.

In the spring and fall I always managed to get a little mud on the cuffs of my Class A uniform pants. That was not necessarily bad. I was always receiving comments like,

"I see you been down to the creek."

"Guys, we better watch out. Lang's been chasing those snaggers."

Maybe I was and maybe I wasn't. But when the time was right I always wanted to leave a smudge of dirt around the cuffs of my pants. I also would do my best to stagger my starting and ending time. If you were an officer worth your salt, you took great joy in keeping the sportsmen guessing.

The Running Fishermen

It was my forty-sixth birthday and four of my fellow officers, my lieutenant, a senior officer, and a couple of new officers, were meeting me for night patrol at Four-Mile Creek to check for illegal trout fishing activities. It was one of those beautiful April nights. The sky was clear and full of stars and the spring peepers were in full chorus. What a night!

I had received some complaints of trout spearing in the streams flowing into Lake Ontario, so we started west and moved east to see what we could find. As we pulled up to Four-Mile Creek, I saw two vehicles and, as I looked across the creek, saw a flash light about one hundred yards from the road.

No matter the situation, my senses always go on high alert when I am in my patrol status mode. We all spread out, the two older officers staying near the

269

road, watching and listening. I proceeded in the direction of the light and, reaching a high area overlooking the creek, saw two individuals with lights and two handheld nets. Usually you have to sit, wait, and watch to find a violation. Not this time. As I watched, one of the men took a swipe with the net and pulled out a large rainbow trout. Bringing it up on land, he quickly brought it over to be admired by his partner. I could hear them talking and a short time later he put the fish under a bush. I left my hiding spot and proceeded towards the two men. The one in the creek saw me and asked,

"Is that you, Jack?"

I spoke real low and said, "Yes."

I was trying to gain some ground on them before they realized it was not Jack. Suddenly they realized I was not Jack and that maybe I was the GAME WARDEN. All of sudden they dropped their nets and were off running.

I yelled, "Conservation Officer, Dick Lang. STOP."

Well, they didn't take my advice and we were off and running in the direction of my lieutenant and the other senior conservation officer. I yelled,

"Grab them, here they come."

Well, no one grabbed them and the fishermen just kept running. I ran right past the officers and then the two men ran across the creek with me in hot pursuit. Well, maybe not that hot!

The last I saw them they were running into a big field of dead goldenrod. Now, dead goldenrod makes a lot of noise, and when it suddenly went quiet, I just knew they were lying in that field. I stopped where I could overlook a large portion of the field. Time went by without anyone moving. What a beautiful night for a chase.

Twenty yards in front of me one of the men got edgy and came up to his knees. Slowly he stood up with his back to me. I said,

"Stop. You are under arrest."

With that, he took off running again. I said to myself,
Enough of this, and yelled,

"Stop or I'll shoot!"

That got his attention! He stopped right away and
raised his hands up in the air. I came up close, spun
him around and found him to be a seventeen-year-old
boy. I said,

"Where's your friend?"

"Somewhere in the field."

"What's his name?"

"Steven."

So I yelled out in a strong, stern voice, "Steven, come over here."

With that, he popped up out of the weeds. I found out he was also 17 years old. With identification of my illegal fish takers completed, we start walking towards the bridge where the vehicles were parked. Moments later the other four officers appeared from their vehicles.

"Here they are, two seventeen year olds."

Officer Case, sensing the chance to rub it in, said,

"So, how do you boys like being caught by a game warden on his forty-sixth birthday?"

Deer Season Opening Day

Opening day was always filled with anticipation and thoughts of another deer, waterfowl, pheasant, or turkey season. But, before opening day, there was all the preparation leading up to that day. From 1976 to 1980 I worked opening day with Officer Dan Ward in Allegheny County. What a change it was going from my territory in Niagara County, where the land was flat and filled with farms, to Allegheny County, with its huge expanse of forest and green foothills leading up to the Allegheny Mountains. It was extremely beautiful. It was a great time to be a conservation officer.

The day before the big day, I would go through a checklist to make sure I had everything I needed: law books, tickets, a flashlight that worked, rope, compass, a change of boots, extra pants, another extra jacket and shirts. I always kept a duffel bag in the trunk filled with the basics but I always double-checked it, just to be sure.

The night before the big day I was trying to get some sleep but everyone in the neighborhood seemed to want to know where Lang lived. Like they didn't already know! Numerous nimrods would use my driveway as a turn-a-round. But I knew better; they were just checking to see if I was at home or out looking for them. To give myself a slight advantage, I would drive my state auto down the driveway, make a left-hand turn, and pull the marked car up tight to my house so those nosey hunters with the red jackets could not find me.

Morning would come before I knew it and I would be on my way to Allegheny County. On my trip down, I would see many vehicles pulled off the highways and many deer hunters scattered about the woods. It was easy to locate them in their bright orange hunting coats. As I approached Allegheny County, I reached out by radio to Officer Ward to coordinate our meeting at his headquarters in Angelica.

Dan showed up with a look of urgency and said,

"Dick, here is a list of townships with the judges names and court dates. I would recommend you start on the Turnpike Road in the town of Almond, where there are a lot of camps. If you need anything, call me on the radio."

I checked the map and was on the Turnpike Road within fifteen minutes. What a coincidence, the first car I stopped was from Niagara County. And they could not believe their eyes!

"Dick Lang! What are you doing down here?"

It threw off all my Niagara County hunters to see me in Allegheny County. I went into my routine.

"Okay, let's open the trunk and check the firearms."

Low and behold, one of their three shotguns was loaded. This was not only dangerous and careless, it was also a serious crime under the conservation law. I couldn't believe it; I had to come all the way to Allegheny County to get a Niagara County hunter in violation of the big game laws.

Every few hours Officer Ward would call to check and see what I was up to. I would always tell him the same thing,

"I'm still on the Turnpike Road and all the violators are from Niagara County!"

It was amazing! By 8:00 PM I still had not left the road and had written seven loaded-gun violations and four tagging violations, all for residents of Niagara County, my home county. From that day forward, Dan and I always referred to the Turnpike Road as "Lang's Road."

The Gun Out The Window

It was the first Saturday of the New York State deer season and I had put in a full day being seen by as many hunters as possible. I decided that evening would be a good time to check for spotlighters, so I got on my state radio and called the Fish & Wildlife Agent in my area, Dan Smoot. Dan was an officer I enjoyed working with and spending hours with in a car telling old game warden stories. He answered me and said he would meet me behind the state barn on the Tonawanda Wildlife Management Area. He jumped in my car bringing his large flashlight. We arrived at the designated spot shortly after sundown. Dan and I worked the Owens Road for a while to see if we would get a spotlighting violation. Driving west, we made a quick right next to a standing cornfield. I turned my state car so it was facing the highway and waited. We were making small talk, listing to radio conversation and watching vehicles go by with nothing happening.

It was forty minutes into our night patrol when a dirty, black van driving east was spotting the south side of the road. Every time you see a light your senses come on high alert. You automatically know where your flashlight is, what side of the vehicle your partner will check, and what you have to do to stay safe. I had found that most of the time the majority of the spotlighters are recreation spotters, not poachers. But, you don't know that until you stop them and you treat each vehicle with the utmost concern for safety. I pulled out easy, giving the van a chance to get about one hundred yards ahead of me. Dan said,

"Hit the lights."

With that, the overhead lights went on. The vehicle went about another 100 yards, with the spotlight bouncing off the passenger side door. Both vehicles came to a stop. I put our spotlight right on his mirror to distract the driver. Dan took the passenger side, I took the driver's.

"Hi guys. Conservation officers; any guns in the vehicle?"

"No Dick, you know we would not have a gun while we are spotting."

We knew better. I did not recognize the passenger but I sure did recognize the driver. Everyone called him Weasel. I always seemed to be just missing him. He had a reputation for taking more deer than his limit, but it was up to me to prove that.

"Okay boys, you mind stepping out? We want to search the vehicle."

We looked that old van over like two good game wardens should, but found nothing. Well, not at that time anyway. We reluctantly said,

"Here is your identification back. Be careful."

We watched the van pull away until it was out of sight, leaving us sitting there.

"What do you think, Dan?"

"I think they had a gun and they threw it out the window."

"Let's walk this shoulder back and see what we find."

Going very slowly and shining our lights back and forth, finally Dan said,

"I have it; here it is."

A nice Remington 12-gauge pump shotgun loaded with three shells. We both started to laugh. Quickly we both got back in the car, turned around and backed into our hiding spot. We wondered how long it was going to take them to come back looking for the gun. Well, it was about twenty minutes and along came the van, going real slow. Now they were right across from us. This is where your people skills come into play.

"Hi guys. Are you looking for this?" I asked, holding up the 12-gauge shotgun where they could see it.

"Oh no Dick, we didn't lose anything."

"Because if you didn't lose this gun, then it must be mine."

They looked at one another for a moment and then decided it was their shotgun. With that, we took the bouncing spotlight and shotgun as evidence, issuing the two spotlighters two tickets each for spotlighting with a firearm in the motor vehicle and possessing a loaded firearm in the vehicle. Weasel moved to Florida shortly thereafter. I heard I had something to do with that decision.

Dick and Officer Dan Ward, 2002

Decoy Deer

I don't know who came up with the idea, but it was a great one. My partner in Genesee County had told me about a mobile decoy deer with a movable head that was managed by electronic controls. What a tool to help apprehend violators that were hard to catch. This would give us a better chance to make an apprehension. It was suggested that I visit the Niagara County Federation to see if they would help finance the purchase of a sitting decoy deer. It would be non-mobile, but it would still look real.

In June of 1997 I made a visit to the Niagara County Sportsmen's Federation meeting held at the Lockport Farm and Home Center. I always enjoyed going to their meetings. This was a group of sportsmen from the local hunting and fishing clubs. They did many things to help fellow sportsmen in the counties across

New York State. They provided the manpower to teach the hunting and trapping courses and were also involved with introducing new legislation. They were always very supportive of law enforcement efforts to help remove the outlaws from the ranks of the legal hunters. I had gone to ask for a donation to purchase a non-mechanical deer decoy and their donation allowed us to purchase our first deer decoy. It was in a sitting position and had a four-point rack.

After we received it, I made plans to work with Environmental Conservation Officer Ron Bosela to check it out. We spent the day checking deer hunters in our own sectors and planned to meet up in the Tonawanda Wildlife Area later in the day to give our decoy its trial run. At 4:00 PM I reached out to Officer Bosela by radio and we agreed to meet in the sportsmen's club parking lot at 5:00 PM. The Wolcottsville Sportsmen's Club was right across the road from the Tonawanda Wildlife Management Area.

At the designated time, Ron drove into the parking lot. We discussed the location, decided Ron would be the pickup car, and I would be the spotter on the Owens Road. I would hide in the pine trees across the road from the decoy. At that time, the decoy had no name, but that was about to change. Officer Bosela was parked about 300 yards to the east of me, waiting for an interested violator.

Twenty minutes into the watch, a slow-moving, full-size Chevrolet came into view. I could see the light bouncing across the field as the vehicle proceeded from east to west. My heart was in my throat as the vehicle stopped right in front of the decoy. The driver's window came slowly down and the long barrel of a shotgun protruded out. The light from the back seat shone on the decoy, a loud report came from the shotgun, and someone in the vehicle yelled,

"It's a DECOY!"

With that, the old Chevy took off as fast as it could. Officer Bosela heard the shot and was ready as they roared past me. Within a mile, I could see the action unfold. Both cars made a quick left at the tee in the road. The old Chevy swerved back and forth as it negotiated the turn, Officer Bosela close behind with his police lights on. I radioed him,

"913 to 924. Is everything okay?"

"Yes," replied Ron, "I have them pulled over in the parking lot at the sportsmen's club."

"I'll be right over," I told him.

Ron met me as I exited my patrol car. There were four of them and they were quite nervous. Officer Bosela held the Remington pump shotgun that he had removed from the passenger side of the car. It was now time to explain what was going to happen. Each passenger would receive two tickets, one for possessing a loaded shotgun in a motor vehicle and one for attempting to take a deer with the aid of an artificial light. I then informed the driver of the vehicle, who was also the shooter, that he held the distinction of being the first to shoot at our decoy and therefore, the decoy would be named after him. The decoy would forever more be called Mikey.

Funny Things

My job was not always serious. There were many occasions when, either by design or by chance, things just happened that turned out to be very humorous.

In 1991, I had my state patrol boat moored next to the Niagara County Sheriff's boat in the hamlet of Olcott. The boat operator for the sheriff's boat was Captain Bruce Wright. Bruce was extremely capable. Whether searching the lake for lost boaters or enforcing the navigation law, Bruce was the best. It was a hot Sunday in July when Bruce heard me sign on the radio.

"ENCON 913 back in service."

"Captain Wright to ENCON Officer Lang. Dick, your boat is taking on water but we have everything under control."

"I am headed that way, I will be there in 20 minutes," I answered.

Ten minutes later he called again.

"Captain Wright to ENCON Officer Lang. Dick your boat is still taking on water but we think we can save it."

What is going on? There was nothing wrong with my boat. I could not believe this was happening. Crossing the bridge of 18-mile Creek I looked down to where my boat should be, but I couldn't see it. Within seconds I was parked and rushing towards the three deputies who were staring into the water. Rounding the corner I looked to where my boat should be and there was no boat. I yelled out in a desperate, high-pitched voice,

"What happened to my boat? I thought everything was okay."

"We tried Dick but we lost it."

"I guess you did."

I looked again down to where my boat should be but all I could see were a life jacket and my radio antenna sticking out of the water. My boat, my boat! I can't believe this.

"I'm sorry, Dick, we tried to save it but we lost it."

All of sudden something clicked in my brain. The antenna was on the wrong side.

"Okay," I said, "where is my boat?"

I looked around and, about 50 yards from where we stood, I saw my boat hidden in among some other boats tied up in the marina.

"You guys almost gave me a heart attack."

They could not stop laughing.

I remember one evening when we were on boat patrol on Lake Ontario and approached a fishing boat that was trolling six lines with only two fishermen on board. At that time there was a limit of two lines per fisherman. We approached the boat and you yelled to the captain, asking how many fishermen were on board. The captain shouted back "THREE" and held up three fingers. You yelled back to go below and get the third fisherman up on deck so we could see him and check their licenses. The captain went below for a minute or so, then returned and yelled "TWO" and held up two fingers. We wrote the captain a ticket for operating too many lines and still chuckle about that when we see each other and hold up three fingers and tell each other "THREE".

Dan Sullivan, Retired ECO.

What Wild Animal Has Bitten You The Most

One of the questions most often asked of me was,

"What wild animal has bitten you the most?"

In my thirty-four years as a conservation officer, I was never bitten by a wild animal. Not a squirrel, not a raccoon, not a coyote, not once. But I have been bitten many times by the family pet, the one that curls up at your feet in the kitchen...your dog. Before I changed into official clothes thirty-four years ago, I had never been bitten by a dog. Then I put on that green uniform, with a gun and Stetson hat and that did it; they all wanted to attack me. I can laugh about it now, but at the time it scared the heck out of me. And, it hurt!

The first time sticks in my head because of the surprise...and the pain. It was a cold Saturday in

November, the first Saturday of the deer season and I was patrolling the Tonawanda Wildlife Area checking deer hunters. At 6:10 PM I received a call from the New York State Police stating that Mrs. Carson, on the Meadville Road, had a deer hunting violation. Great. I was about a mile from her home as the crow flies and I was hoping it was a good complaint. Driving south on the Meadville Road I looked for a house with a porch light on. Sure enough, I found it. A woman came to the door and I introduced myself.

"Hi, Mrs. Carson, Dick Lang, Conservation Officer. The state police said you have a complaint for me."

"Yes, come on in."

As I followed her to the kitchen to get a statement, I passed the couch, and, all of a sudden, felt a sharp pain in the back of my left leg. I let out a loud "Yeow!" or some other incoherent word and turned around to see this small mongrel dog glaring at me. It never barked, just snuck out from behind the couch and let me have it on the back of my left calf.

"Did she bite you?"

"You're darn right she bit me."

"You dirty cur," she yells. "She's never done that before."

Yea, that's what all the owners say.

With that, she grabbed a two by four piece of lumber, swung it over her head and brought it down on the animal's head and back.

"There, she won't do that again."

The dog knew she had done something wrong and slunk back under the couch.

"Ma'am, does that dog have its rabies shots?"

"Oh yes, Mr. Lang, I'll show you the certificate."

She opened a small drawer, the type we all have, a junk drawer, with all kinds of crap in it, all those things we think we are going to use some day but never do. Things were flying in all directions, but no certificate. Ten minutes went by.

"I know it's in here somewhere, but I can't seem to find it."

"Mrs. Carson, I have to go. Here is my card with my phone number. When you find that rabies certificate, please call my home and tell my wife."

I left and never pulled into my own driveway until 10:50 PM. I had just closed the door of my patrol car and headed to the house when my wife ran out yelling,

"Are you okay, are you okay? This lady called and said you do not need to go the hospital because she found the rabies certificate. Are you okay? What happened?"

She sure got my wife all worked up. I quickly explained that I had been bitten by her small dog. It turned out that this was just the first of many dogs who took a liking to my legs!

Maybe it was the uniform. An acquaintance of mine who was a schoolteacher and farmer had a problem with an archery hunter who was trespassing on his farm. I pulled into Henry's driveway, exited the car and proceeded towards the house. Henry came out of his new barn and called,

"Come back here, Dick."

294

Well, his dog saw me and started barking and running towards me. It was a German shorthaired pointer and he looked awfully big to me. Well, you know the thought that was going through my mind. But, just in case you don't, here it is. I thought, *He's going to bite me*. I always tried to give good vibes to dogs saying, *It's okay, I'm your buddy*. But, I guess some dogs just don't get it. This one ran full tilt into me, biting me on the right thigh, and tearing my class A uniform pants. I thought, *What did I do to deserve this*? Harold asked,

"Did he bite you?"

"Yes he bit me."

"He's never done that before."

Where have I heard that before?

"It must have been the uniform."

Well, whatever it was, I was bitten again.

One of the last times I was bitten by a dog was because of a business complaint. I had received a complaint of possible illegal rabbit hunting on the Tierney Construction property in the Town of Lockport. I was running a little late, which I hate to do, and Ray came outside to greet me with his big old German shepherd.

"Hi Ray, what's the complaint?"

"Well Dick, it's a trespasser."

All this time the dog has not barked, growled, or been anything but pleasant.

"Hi pup, how's it going," I said as I patted it on the head.

"Come on inside and I will give you the license plate number."

I followed Ray and the dog into the office. The information was good and we continued to talk as I exited the building. The dog had followed me out of the office and started to smell my left leg when all of a sudden it bit me hard, breaking through the skin on my thigh.

I yelled, and thought it was a good thing I had my insulated underwear on, because this dog hammered me.

"Did he bite you?" Damn right he bit me. I was not a happy camper.

"He's never done that before."

Yea, sure!

"It must be the uniform and the gun."

Here we go again.

"Let's see your rabies certificate."

I ended up at Lockport hospital for a tetanus shot, which Ray kindly paid for. Maybe it was the uniform...again!

These are just a few of the many dog encounters that came my way during my thirty-four year career. It was not that I disliked dogs because I didn't. Normally I have a great relationship with dogs. I have owned many a hunting dog and never had a problem until I put that uniform on. Then those dogs saw red and I saw the hospital ER.

The Deer in the Tree

It was opening day of deer season in 1987 and I was patrolling the back roads in the town of Royalton. Driving down the Mann Road I noticed a small buck deer hanging in a tree. That is not so unusual but it opens the door for a game warden to check a deer tag. Approaching the house, I knocked a few times and a woman opened the door.

"Can I help you?" she asked.

"Yes, Dick Lang, Conservation Officer, and I would like to check the deer."

"Sure, go ahead."

It was a 4-point buck and I was in luck; I could reach the tag in the deer's ear. A Becky Wrangler's name was on the tag.

"Are you Becky?"

"Yes."

Well, I looked at her and thought to myself, *She didn't shoot that deer, her husband did.* But, I decided to play along and see what I could find out.

"Becky, where did you shoot the deer?"

"Behind the house."

"Would you please put your boots on and show me where you shot this buck?"

Moments later we were headed to a small wood lot behind the ranch house. I noticed that we seemed to be walking in circles, but I decided to give her some time. I noticed another bad habit; she kept looking in the tops of trees for the gut pile of a deer. No way deer fly. Finally I said,

"Becky, I think it's time you were honest with me and tell me who shot this deer. We have walked around here long enough looking up into the trees. There are no deer in the trees and you did not shoot that deer."

We stopped walking and there was a long pause before she said,

"My husband shot the deer and used my tag."

"I kind of figured that."

We never did find the gut pile, but she got a ticket for lending her license to another, and her husband got one for failing to tag. The story got back to me that all the local husbands in this area started showing their wives where the gut pile was so if Lang came looking they could show him where the deer was killed. It made quite the story for a few years. Know where the gut pile is and don't bother looking in the trees for it!

Indian Complaints

I had just come home for dinner in October 1991 and heard the phone ringing as I came up the front steps. I heard my wife say,

"Yes Herb, he'll be right here."

"Hi Herb," I said, "I haven't heard from you in a while. What's going on?"

"Ken Solaris, the dairy farmer whose land butts up to the Indian reservation, is complaining that those darn Indians are going on his property and killing deer. He hears them shooting at all hours of the night. Can you come over and help catch them?"

"I will get hold of Neil Ross, and Lieutenant Bob Kauffman."

I called Neil, explained the situation to him, and arranged to meet him and Herb the next night at 8:00 PM at the deli. Herb got there first and crawled in the back seat of my state car. Herb is not a big guy, but you could always recognize him by his voice; it was on the squeaky side. Neil pulled up next and joined Herb in the back seat. Herb gave directions and we proceeded down Slayton Settlement Road to the Solaris farm. I asked if we needed to let the family know what we were doing, but Neil said he had it all taken care of. As I drove past the barn I could see the cows in the stanchions waiting to be milked. I drove slowly down the farm lane, watching the potholes, and pulled under some trees where we had a good view in the direction of the reservation. It was a beautiful night. It was clear, about 45 degrees, with a sky full of stars.

As we were making small talk, Bob looked up and saw a light bouncing off the treetops. We figured they might be looking for raccoons. The truck pulled into the field and stopped, leaving its headlights on. Herb chimed in,

"They're off the reservation."

I counted three individuals on the bed of the flatbed truck. A hand-held light was shining all around. In our car we were all watching intently, with Herb jabbering away. Suddenly...bang, bang, bang, bang, bang. They were shooting off the bed of the truck. But shooting at nothing, just shooting up into the air, up into the trees, everywhere. We all felt there were three guns, rifles, not shotguns. Time went by. If there had been any deer around they were gone now. We watched them for what seemed like an hour, but was probably only about 20 minutes. Finally I said,

"It's time to go. Let's see if we can surprise them."

Pulling out of the hedgerow, with our car lights out, I slowly crept across the field, which I had never seen or been in before. I couldn't believe they hadn't taken off by now. Maybe they still didn't know we were there. I drove to within 50 yards of them, thinking that maybe I could make it to the truck without them seeing me. Within seconds I was there. I turned on the overhead lights and the headlights and what confusion! We jumped out of the car yelling,

"Conservation officers. You're under arrest for having loaded guns on a motor vehicle."

The words did not come out of my mouth very well. When I turned my lights on and looked ahead I was ten feet from driving into a pond. I know there was someone looking after me that night. The look on those Indians' faces when we jumped out the car was priceless. They were so confused!

We took their guns, unloading and collecting shells, writing tickets and giving receipts for the firearms and shells. What a night. Herby would not shut up about how we finally got those poaching Indians. I was just thankful I did not drive in the pond. All I could see was the huge amount of paper work I would be filling out.

The Easiest Ticket I Ever Wrote

It was a beautiful October day and I had what I thought was a day off. I planned to rake the leaves off the front lawn. As I headed from the garage to the front of the house I noticed a pickup truck turning into my driveway. I looked up to see if it was anyone I recognized.

"Hi guys. How can I help you?"

"Are you Dick Lang, the game warden?"

"Yes I am. What happened to bring you guys over here?"

"Well, we were hunting ducks off Rt. 77 in the Tonawanda Wildlife Area and we ended up going where we shouldn't have. Then a guy in a green pickup truck came down the dike and told us we were hunting in a prohibited area. We didn't know it, but he pointed out a sign that said the area was closed to hunting. He then asked to see our hunting licenses and he wrote down our names and address. He said he would be getting hold of an Officer Lang and he would contact us. I said to Mac,

"You know where Lang lives don't you?"

"Yea, he lives about five miles from here on the way to Lockport."

"So, we decided to get this over with."

"Well, gentlemen, it looks like you were trespassing in a prohibited area of the Tonawanda Wildlife Area. Why don't you give me your hunting licenses and I will call the wildlife technician to confirm what happened."

Just my luck, I found him back at the permit station and he confirmed what had happened. I headed back to my patrol car where I located my ticket book. It did not take long before I had finished the charge and handed them back their hunting licenses and a ticket. I give them instructions on where to appear for court. As they pulled out of the driveway, I took hold of the leaf rake and headed for the front lawn again, thinking that those were two of the easiest tickets I had ever given.

308

The Growth of Fishing in Lake Ontario

It was the 1970s and fishing in the western basin of Lake Ontario was at its lowest point. Detergents, chemicals and the lamprey eel had all contributed to the demise of our lake fishing. The blue pike had disappeared in both Lake Erie and Lake Ontario. I found it hard to believe that I could drive to a community on Lake Ontario and not see anyone fishing. How could that be? Thank goodness the DEC Fisheries personnel had the foresight to clean up the lakes by treating the breeding streams with the necessary chemicals to kill the lamprey larva. Then, new laws were passed that changed the makeup of detergents, eliminating the phosphates. Finally, DEC Fisheries Department introduced brown trout, lake trout, Coho salmon, and King salmon. The fishing resumed slowly. I remember there was a learning experience to determine which lure to use, the depth to use it at, and the water temperature that would indicate at what level those big King salmon would be found.

Many of our western New York fishermen had been going to the state of Michigan for trout and salmon fishing in Lake Michigan and Lake Huron and this experience may have given them an edge. But New York's trout and salmon regulations were quite liberal at this time. You could take five fish a day, snagging was allowed, and you could fish 24 hours a day. What more could you ask for.

My first salmon fishing derby in Lake Ontario was an eye-opening experience. I had placed a call to ECO Frank Lohr, from Franklinville, to see if he would assist me with my first derby. He showed up at my residence, ready to go, at 3:30 AM on Thursday, the first day of the tournament. As we traveled north to the hamlet of Olcott, I asked Officer Lohr many questions about downriggers and other equipment. I had no idea what to expect. As I turned the corner onto Route 18, I could not believe my eyes. If I had not known where Lake Ontario was, I would have thought I was looking at a small city; there were so many boat lights in front of us. We parked, got in our patrol boat, exited the harbor and began to check fishing boats for violations. We were checking for licenses, too many lines, and any navigation law violations.

For me it was an overwhelming experience to see all those fishing boats in Lake Ontario. What a success story for the Fisheries unit of the New York State Environmental Conservation Department. If you enjoyed fishing, this was the place to be. I felt like I was in the old west. People were here from all over the U.S. and the salmon and trout did not let them down.

One of the greatest memories I have of fishing Lake Ontario was in 1989. My two sons, Michael, home from college, and John, home from his job on a cruise ship in Hawaii, asked if I knew anyone who would take them fishing. I had an idea and called ECO Matt Pestinger. He agreed to take us out on his new personal boat.

Meeting in Youngstown at the designated time, Matt and his five passengers, myself, my two sons, and two friends, headed for Lake Ontario. Fishing a mile off shore in 150 feet of water was just right. Matt did a great job of trolling when one of the downriggers went off. Fish on, John grabbed the pole and, after a fifteen-minute fight, a six-pound Coho salmon was in the box. It was the first of five to be caught that day. As you can see by all the smiles, it was a great day of fishing.

John Lang, Matt Pestinger, Matt's friend,
Mike Lang, Dave Keltch
Early 1990s

The Kid and His History Book

All environmental conservation officers have a few cases that really stick out in their memory and my next case was one of those.

It was April of 1982 and I had checked a group of teenage boys spearing suckers in 12-Mile Creek. The bag contained a few suckers, but none of the three boys had a fishing license. It was always our decision when to go easy and when to get really tough, so I said,

"Boys, I'm going to give you a break this time. As long as you purchase a fishing license and send it to me, I will not issue a ticket. But, if you don't send it within a week, I will be over and issue you a ticket."

Of course, I scared the crap out of two of the boys, but the third one was going to push my buttons. I had his phone number and called him a week later. His mother answered the phone. I explained about her son spearing without a license and told her I was giving him a break if he would purchase a license and send it to me. If he failed to do so, I told her, I could have a warrant issued for his arrest. With that, she became very belligerent.

"Leave the kid alone. Go catch someone who committed a murder. You can't write tickets anyway; you're not a real policeman."

With that she hung up. Now, normally it takes a lot to make me mad, but she had managed to do it! I went down to Judge Moxham in the Town of Wilson for an arrest warrant. I had never asked for a warrant for a 17-year old, but this one was pushing the limits. My plan was to go to the Niagara Falls High School and pick him up from school instead of chasing him and his mother around.

At 1:30 PM I arrived at the school, identified myself, and asked to see the principal. Moments later he appeared and walked me to his office. I told him what had happened and why I was there. Checking his class roster he called the boy's history teacher and asked that the boy be sent to his office. When he walked in, the principal explained why I was there. This time the kid didn't give me any trouble. I thanked the principal for his assistance and escorted the young man out to my car. Driving to Wilson, I asked if his mother was available by phone. He just shook his head, no.

Arriving at the judge's home, we proceeded to her office where she looked over the paperwork and asked the defendant how he wanted to plead. He informed the judge that he didn't have any money and that he couldn't get hold of his mother, but that he was guilty as charged. With that, the judge said,

"I'm not going to babysit the kid. Take him to jail. Here is the paperwork; take him to Lockport."

As we drove out of the driveway, I told him that this could have been handled much differently if he had only gotten a fishing license like his buddies. *And, if your mother had listened,* I thought to myself. As we pulled in the parking lot of the Niagara County jail, I picked up his history book and turned him over to the booking officer. I couldn't help but think about the lesson to be learned by a 17-year-old, or anyone, when he heard the CLANK of that big steel door close behind him.

Dick, you and I spent many hours, days and nights together, but one of the most important time was one you don't remember. It was the day I spent riding with you when I was in college. It was a great day for me and it reinforced my already strong desire to become a conservation officer. Now I can say that I'm retired from a job that always was and still is my dream job. Thanks, Dick.

Dan Sullivan, Retired ECO.

The Early Goose

It was a Sunday, and Monday was opening day of the waterfowl season. I was patrolling the Tonawanda Wildlife Area looking for any illegal activity. I had stopped in the parking lot to give some information to a group of small game hunters when the state police radio caught my attention.

"Lockport to ENCON 7N913. Call your headquarters (home) for a complaint."

I searched for a phone at the DEC barn in the refuge area and called my wife. The wives of conservation officers double as secretaries, reference sources, organizers and surrogate parents of orphaned wildlife.

"Hi," I said, "what's up?"

My wife said a farmer had shot a goose, even though the season was closed. I knew the location and knew it would take about 30 minutes to get there. Arriving at the farm, I knocked on the door and a skinny, young man in overhauls answered my knock.

"Hi Mr. Hobbs. Dick Lang, Conservation Officer."

"What can I do for you?"

"I am here regarding the goose you shot."

"I didn't shoot a goose."

"Well, let's take a look around."

I could see loose goose feathers floating around the driveway in front of the barn. I could not believe it. It was less than an hour and he had the goose plucked already.

"Karl, where is the goose? All I need are those feathers and I have enough information to give you a ticket."

"Alright, follow me and I'll give you the goose."

He had an upstairs apartment with an outside set of stairs. As he opened the door I could see a big pot steaming on the stove. I said,

"I take it that's the goose."

"Yea."

I removed the cover and, sure enough, there was the illegal goose.

"Karl, do you have a box or basket I can put the goose in? I need it for evidence."

A moment later he produced a cardboard box that was just the right size. Removing the goose from the boiling hot water, I found it hard to believe that less than one hour ago this Canadian goose was flying free with a flock of geese and now was in the cook pot. I gave Jim a receipt and a ticket for taking a Canadian goose during the closed season.

It was great, I loved my job. I wanted to be a game warden since I met Ted Strang when I was ten, and he took me fishing in Lake Erie. I was so fortunate to have the job I loved, I loved working with people. But it is different now, I think that to a lot of guys it's just a job.

Harry Keppner, Retired ECO.

The Ever-Changing Wildlife Scene

Niagara County has always been blessed with an abundance of wild fish, birds and animals. Large flocks of migratory Canadian geese visited our ponds and cut cornfields, but some of our locals thought it was their God-given right to take a few spring geese. It was one of those frustrating things that, for all the hours I put into trying to make an apprehension, I got very few arrests, though not for lack of trying. Despite the number of Canadian geese that were taken, I am sure that I did have an impact on reducing the illegal hunting of migratory Canadian geese.

You have to remember that these people were not proud of what they did and would do everything they could to cover their actions. They would hide in the bushes, hide in a barn or shoot out of the second story of a house. On many a cloudy day, about two hours before sunset, I would set up where I could see a field of winter wheat. The geese would be making so much noise and then I would hear the blast of a shotgun two roads to the north. The geese all disappeared. It was very frustrating to say the least. This was one of those rural family traditions handed down from grandfather to son and then to grandson. Then in the 1990's the Canadian goose population exploded and the tradition faded away.

On the Easter break, oh boy did those boys give me a run for my money. It seemed that no fish or bird was sacred. The rainbow trout were in the feeder streams off Lake Ontario and the stream was not only filled with fish but boys with nets, fishing poles and spears. They always kept an eye out for my green state car. It didn't matter if I was in a car with a state shield on the door or in an unmarked car; they did their best to know where I was.

Then there were the BB guns and .22 rifles. The songbirds were fair game to any sixteen-year-old with an open field next to his house. These boys were not as hard to catch as the goose shooters. I hate to say it but, since the introduction of the computer, I see fewer boys doing any kind of outdoor activity.

The tradition of spearing the spring suckers was something I was unfamiliar with, but I sure leaned about it in a hurry. On a clear night with the temperature in the 50s and the spring peepers making their beautiful music, my partner, Kimpton Vosburg, would call and say, "Let's check some spearers tonight." The first time it happened, I thought, okay I've heard about this but I've not seen it. Let's do it.

"Where do you want to meet?" I asked.

"Meet you in Wilson at the town hall at 8:00PM."

"Okay, see you there."

Wilson is a town on 12-Mile Creek and many small feeder streams harbor suckers, northern pike and the occasional rainbow trout. Taking the passenger seat in Vossy's unmarked, black Dodge we came to a bridge in the village where I had seen cars parked and lights bobbing along the creek. We quietly closed the doors of the patrol car and walked in the direction of the lanterns, carrying our flashlights but keeping them turned off. I got my first introduction to spearing. It was a very interesting way to harvest fish. One fisherman would stand in the stream with hip boots on, spear in one hand, flashlight in the other and with a burlap bag attached to his belt with bailing twine. As long as we were quiet, we could follow them at a close enough distance that we could see and hear everything. One thing that was to our advantage was that their lanterns cast a light that only allowed them to see directly in front of them. We would step up next to the creek and introduce ourselves, asking to check their fishing licenses. Then we would check their bag for suckers or who knows what kind of fish we might find. It could be a northern pike or a trout.

Judge Clive Merritt, a farmer, and the owner of the local metal shop, was the local gossip stop for all the police in the area. While there you could have your arrest warrant signed and hear the many stories Clive had to tell about growing up in the early 1900's on a subsistence farm spearing fish in the ditches. It was a tradition of the local families, not for recreation but because it was a necessity. Clive's evening chore was spearing suckers.

His favorite way of preserving them was to can them in boiling water. One day he gave me a jar.

"Here, Dick, take a jar home for you and your wife."

It did not sound good to me, but I thanked him as I accepted the jar. When I got home, I told my wife,

"Honey, Clive gave me a jar of canned suckers. We have to try them."

We opened the jar and were hit with a smell that told us were probably not going to like this. But, wanting to be gracious, we each gave that jar of canned suckers a quick taste, then said good-by to the rest. Oh well. By the early 1990's sucker spearing had became illegal.

About the same time that sucker spearing was going on I was introduced to another fishing activity that was new to me, smelt dipping. Smelt are a small, slim, tasty fish that showed up in great numbers in the lower Niagara River and would reach their peak around mid-April. I was fortunate enough to have seen the large schools of smelt before they all but disappeared. Smelt were taken by dip netting off the Lewiston Sand Dock pier or along the shoreline in the Artpark State Park. The word would get out that the smelt were in, get your bucket and dip net and make sure you have your fishing license.

I would call my partner, Kimpton Vosburg, who knew the river like no one else and was an expert at teaching me the ins and outs of smelt dipping. Being young and enthusiastic, I wanted to do and see every possible activity. Standing among the smelt dippers I felt like I was in a small city of lanterns. There was very little talking, just the swish of the net hitting the water. Then the smelt would come up into the light. One good dip and you could fill a bucket. We would then start checking fishing licenses.

Fishermen came from towns that were very close and as far away as Rochester. I would always get a few "no licenses" from Rochester. I would then call Justice Jowdey from Cambria, because he was on the way back to Rochester on Route 104. Around 11:30 PM I would say good night to Officer Vosburg, round up my Rochester smelt-dippers and give them instructions on where the justice lived. I called ahead and Justice Jowdey was always waiting for me and my violators. Like most of the judges, he had an office in his home so he could accommodate the different police agencies after office hours. Entering Judge Jowdey's office was like going back into the late 1800's. He had an old roll-top desk, and pictures of President Washington and President Lincoln on the wall. The last item that made the room perfect was a potbelly stove and, of course, it was already creating a warmth that made everyone comfortable. It was always pleasant for me to visit Judge Jowdey.

There are still small numbers of smelt but nothing like there were. There are many nights when, despite your best efforts, none will enter your dip net. After the introduction of lake trout, King salmon, steelhead, and Coho salmon, the smelt population has been greatly reduced. The smelt is now the food fish for the larger predatory fish such as the thirty-five-pound salmon.

Another bird that has almost disappeared from our Niagara County landscape is the pheasant. I almost cry when I say the word. I was brought up on pheasant hunting. That is where I got my love of the outdoors from, hunting pheasant with my dad in Orchard Park. When I turned 16 I would get off the school bus, grab the 16-gauge Browning, my trio of beagles and head for the fields that surrounded the Lang home. Fast forward to the 1970's in Niagara County. I was now a N.Y.S. Conservation Officer with a house in the country. Pheasants were still everywhere and my Brittany spaniel would hunt with me. What more could I ask for? Well, after only five years on the job, the pheasant population took a sharp drop and by the mid 1980's had all but disappeared. It's such a shame. What a thrill to hear and see this majestic bird crowing as it was exploding in front of you from under a point by your bird dog.

I do not believe that hunting is what reduced their numbers. My belief is that it was the explosion of predators, both flying and ground. The protection of hawks and owls both in New York and nationwide helped contribute to the reduction of pheasants, along with the increase in the ground nesting predators such as raccoons, fox, coyotes, skunks, and opossums. With all these predators, how can a wild pheasant possibly survive? They don't. My grandsons will never have the thrill of seeing a rooster exploding out of the grass, soaring up right under their guns.

Region 9, late 1990s
Dick is fifth from left in back row

Things Were Not Always Serious

My job was not always serious. Many times I had enough comical things happen to keep me laughing and shaking my head.

I remember one especially funny waterfowl opener. The season opened on Saturday, a half-hour before sunrise. It depended on the weather, but it was usually still dark when the season opened. That was easy for me to say, there are many degrees of dark. The week before the season was to open, I contacted Officer Dan Sullivan. What a great officer. I always tried to get Dan to help me out during duck season or down in the Niagara River when the salmon were in. Dan had an easygoing personality and a calming voice. He agreed to meet me at 5:00AM at my house.

I always had a restless night's sleep before the opening of duck season. I had so many things on my mind...what's the weather going to be like, will the other officers show up? I was finishing breakfast when Dan drove in. We attached the canoe on top of the car and were off for the swamp. We approached the state game management area, which had the look of a small city. We didn't see many people but there were cars everywhere. After a drive around the area, we decided to put in off the Owens Road. We put on our cover jackets and hip boots and picked up our shotguns. As we pushed off, we saw hunters hiding everywhere. We headed to the north dike when, all of a sudden, a shot rang out. It was like the start of a NASCAR Race. One shot and every hunter in the swamp started shooting. Now that everyone was shooting, we stopped to watch and see what fell from the sky.

It just so happened that there were a lot of coots in the marsh that fall. The change in the weather had driven them south and they stopped here to take a break on their long trip. I told Dan,

"Dan, these guys to the east of us have been shooting at those coots. I think they would be a good check."

As we canoed over to them, they looked confused.

"Hi guys. Conservation officers. We would like to check your ducks, firearms and licenses."

Then I understood why they looked confused; they were five Greek men from the city of Buffalo. You could tell they enjoyed hunting, but how much they knew about waterfowl hunting was something else. Dan found an unplugged shotgun and a hunting license violation. The one hunter with the bandoleer across his chest had a pile of coots in front of him. I asked him,

"Do you enjoy eating coots?"

"Oh yes, they are very good."

It was time to head to the road where we could finish up this case. With licenses and coots in hand, we headed back with our hunters in tow. As we finished our paper work one of the duck hunters sauntered over to me and asked,

"Do you like coot?"

I could not resist. I replied,

"Sure I like coot."

"How do you fix them?"

Dan was now listening intently, wondering what I was going to say next. I had the feeling I had my duck hunter hooked so I answered,

"There is only one way to fix coots. I put a pan of water on the stove and bring it to a boil. Then I put my coot in the water, adding basil, salt, pepper and oregano. Next I put the lid on and leave it to cook for thirty minutes. I check under the lid after fifteen minutes and, oh boy, was that coot smelling good. After thirty minutes, it's time for the coot to come out."

I could not believe I still had their attention. No one seemed to have caught on. So, I continued,

"I take the coot out of the cooking pot and place it on a plate. After taking a good look, I decide to throw away the coot and eat the plate."

Officer Sullivan broke out laughing and my coot hunter, with a strange look in his eye, said,

"You tell a joke." I decided I could not let this go on any longer.

"Yes, I am telling a joke."

They really did not get it but Sully and I laugh every time one of us brings up the word coot.

Patrol Boat, 2000

Four-Wheel Drive

It was 1995 and the drivers of trucks with four-wheel-drive and lots of horsepower seemed to be on a quest to conquer the Tonawanda Wildlife Area. They thought they were invincible and had already destroyed large areas of plant life and rutted up the area. I knew it was just a matter of time before I would find one stuck.

It was going on 6:30 PM on May 16th and I had decided to patrol the Tonawanda Wildlife Area. This area had been purchased by the New York State Conservation Department in the 1960s as a waterfowl management area. It was flat, with manmade potholes. For the last month, we had had our share of rain and the ducks and geese were everywhere, bobbing for food in the roadside ditches. The drive-by shooters were also everywhere, taking a whack at Canadian geese or Mallard Ducks.

Making a left turn on the Bartell Road, I saw what I believed to be a truck up ahead. It looked a bit lopsided and was sitting lower than I was used to seeing them. Then I saw why. That beautiful four-wheel-drive truck was stuck right up to the running boards. I stopped my patrol car and approached the truck cautiously, expecting to find the owner. But, there was no owner to be found. I inspected the vehicle and found it to be locked. What a sight, that beautiful new truck, all mud-spattered and unable to move.

I knew what the drivers had been thinking. *We can go anywhere. This truck is invincible.*

I placed a call to the State Police in Lockport asking for a vehicle check. Moments later the police called back and reported that the owner's location was within three miles of his truck. Within moments I was at his home, knocking on the door.

"Hi, Pete. Dick Lang, Conservation Officer. I found your truck stuck in a prohibited area of the Tonawanda Wildlife Area."

"I knew you were coming. What took you so long?"

"What do you mean?"

"Well, once I got stuck I said to my buddy, I hope Lang isn't working tonight."

"Well, I am and I need your driver's license."

After issuing him a ticket for driving in a prohibited area and giving him instructions on pulling the vehicle out, I continued my patrol of the state lands.

The Ice Fishing Check

It was a crisp, cold Wednesday in February of 2003 when I exited my green sedan at the Wilson Harbor. There, in front of me, were eighteen small pop-up tents dotted all over the ice. Grabbing my warm gloves and my muskrat cap, I shut the door and headed to the first hut to check the fishing license, the species of fish, and to be sure the name and address was on each tip up.

As I came to the first hut, I heard a couple of individuals talking. By now they had figured out that Dick Lang was here and they started digging for their fishing licenses. And I do mean digging for them. It's cold, very cold, and they're all layered in coats, coveralls and insulated long johns. These first men checked out okay, just had a couple of sunfish, and I was off in the direction of a single individual sitting on a plastic five-gallon pail.

"Hi, how's the fishing? Could I check your fishing license?"

"I live on the reservation."

"That's great, you don't need a New York State fishing license as long as you produce an Indian ID Card."

Taking his gloves off, he reached into his shirt pocket and produced his Tuscarora Indian Identification Card. Verifying that in fact this was Harold Reddick, I handed back the card. Continuing to make small talk, I started to inspect his tip ups for name and address. This was an old law, used to show ownership. As I inspected the five tip ups claimed by Mr. Reddick, I noticed there was no name or address on any of them.

"Harold, where is your name and address?"

"Oh I don't need that, I'm an Indian."

"Yes, I know you're an Indian, but that policy is only good for fishing licenses, it does not exempt you from the other areas of the Conservation Law."

I asked Mr. Reddick for his driver's license and proceeded to issue him a ticket for failing to have his tip up properly identified with his name and address. With that, he started quoting different treaties that were signed by the Iroquois Confederacy and the United States government or New York State back in the late 1700s and early 1800s. I proceeded to give him the ticket, explaining when he was to appear in court. He continued to say that this was not fair and he would plead not guilty.

"That is your right if you so desire."

I filed my portion of the ticket away in my ticket book with all the pertinent information. Shortly after the court night had come and gone, I received a notice in the mail stating that Harold Reddick had pleaded not guilty and was requesting a trial. At the end of March the trial convened. I was in Wilson Town Court in my class A dress uniform, representing New York State, without an attorney.

Mr. Reddick took issue with the fact that he had to comply with the New York Conservation Law because he was an Indian. I took the position that the only exception was the fact that his identification card was his fishing or hunting license when he came off the reservation. That did not grant him special permission to exceed the limit of fish or game or to disobey regulations on equipment to be used.

After Judge Robert Botzer heard the arguments he found Mr. Reddick guilty of failing to put his name and address on each of his tip ups.

"That will be $25 dollars. Do you have that Mr. Reddick?"

Harold dug in his pocket and brought out a twenty and a five-dollar bill. As we parted, he still insisted he was right and that he was going to appeal it to the county court. I was thinking, *Sure. Do you know how many people have told me that over my thirty-four-year career?*

Two years came and went and I had an opportunity to come into contact with the town of Royalton's Attorney, Tom Brandt.

"Dick, was that your case with the Indian in court for not having his name and address on the tip ups?"

"Yes, that was my case. What's going on with it?"

"Well, he appealed it to county court where the decision was the same. Then, he appealed it again, this time to the New York State Court of Appeals and he was still found guilty."

But, there was still one last place he could appeal to, the United States Supreme Court in Washington, D.C., and that's just what he did. Niagara County Assistant District Attorney Tom Brandt knew of my interest in the case and kept me informed. I was hoping the Supreme Court would hear it, because I would be there in a minute to witness the proceedings. How many officers go through their entire career without any of their cases going to the U.S. Supreme Court? Another period of time went by and I received a call from ADA Thomas Brandt.

"Dick, you can cancel your plans to go to Washington. The Supreme Court will not hear the case. The decision of the Wilson court stands, guilty.

I was disappointed, but I knew I still had set a precedent in New York State Environmental Conservation Law. Who would have thought that checking a Native American ice fisherman in the Wilson Harbor on a cold day in February would result in a case that would end up in the U.S. Supreme Court? Well, mine did.

Dick and Federal Agent Dan Smoot

Car-Killed Deer

Highway-killed deer were a common occurrence for a conservation officer. The practice of picking up every car-killed deer had just changed in 1969 when I joined the force. Prior to that date, the game protectors/conservation officers picked up deer and disposed of them. In 1969 a new policy became effective and the highway departments picked up dead deer during their normal working hours. It was much easier for them to pick them up and dispose of them, burying what was left. Sometimes they would take a piece of equipment to the scene and bury it right along the highway. We were still supposed to pick up deer on weekends, holidays, and after hours.

Conservation officers always spoke of road-killed deer with disdain. Everyone had an opinion about all the deer meat you would get back from the processor, but for the most part, you would be very disappointed. The older officers would do everything they could to get out of picking up a deer. We had no place to put them other than on the trunk of the state car and ended up with blood oozing everywhere. And, of course, it stank. I usually ended up going on these complaints alone. There was no use in calling another officer, he was out having fun and here I was, stuck with this dead deer. The older officers would offer advice and told me time and again, watch how you lift that deer 'cause you'll screw up your back.

I remember one September when the trees were especially beautiful, glowing with that beautiful gold and red color. I was home eating supper when the phone rang.

"Dick, there is a big buck on Lincoln Road Extension causing a traffic problem. Can you take a look at it?"

"Okay. I'll be down as soon as I finish supper."

I finished the wonderful supper my wife had prepared for me, then headed out to get the dead deer. I only had to go down to Lincoln Avenue, so I figured it shouldn't take me too long. Sure enough, there it was, a nice 8-point buck lying on the shoulder of the road. *Gosh*, I thought, *that must have done a lot of damage to the vehicle.* But there wasn't any vehicle in sight. I went to the trunk and pulled out my deer line. First I tried to horse him onto the car by pulling his head and front legs, but only got him as far as the bumper. Next I tried dragging him up by the back legs. No good, he is too heavy. My next thought was that I was going to need help and hoped a Good Samaritan would stop and help me throw this stinky dead deer up on my trunk. Time went by and people were slowing down to watch me, but no one stopped. I could not believe this. I had been here 20 minutes and obviously looked like I needed help, but no one has offered.

"*That's it*," I finally decided. I took out my half-inch manila line and tied it around the neck of this 8-point buck and then to the trailer hitch on the state car. This sure won't hurt my back and it sure is going to lower the weight of this buck, so maybe I could handle it. I had just the spot for this deer. On the state wildlife area, six miles away, there was a pit used to dump the carcasses of any wildlife from deer, to raccoon to muskrats, and that was where this animal was going.

I started off slowly, then picked up speed when I could hear the deer bouncing along behind me. The deer was leaving a stain on the highway and he was becoming a lot lighter as I approached the pit. By the time I got there, the deer was no more than one layer of fur and skin, everything else was on the highway. But, two good things happened. Number one, I had removed a driving hazard, and number two, no less important, I saved my back.

As my career came to a close the conservation officers had gotten completely away from picking up car-killed deer. They either stayed rotting along the highway or the highway departments removed them. It is a rare occasion now that an environmental conservation officer's police car is seen with a deer across the trunk.

How Things Have Changed

I cannot believe the changes I have seen in my 34-year career. When I was a young officer checking small game hunters in Niagara County, it was a very different place. The fall, especially, was a wonderful time of year. There were special sights and sounds that made me feel alive. The wind blowing a stiff breeze from the north would bring in those large billowy clouds and put a nip in the air. Exiting the car I would be greeted by the high-pitched sound of large flocks of starlings migrating on their way south. Then I would hear the Mallards quacking and the Wood Ducks making their own distinct noise, and I knew I was in the best place on earth. But it's changing.

During the 1960s and '70s the wild pheasant population was very stable in all the counties along Lake Ontario. Niagara County was the number one pheasant-hunting county in the state. Hunters came from all over New York and from out of state to hunt pheasants. Pheasants are not only beautiful to see, but also wonderful to hear. It's a great feeling to hear a rooster crowing in a hay field on a quiet spring day. And, what a sight to see a mature rooster courting a hen with his ear standing up and his red face glistening in the sun. In the fall, my dog and I would take a quick hunt behind the house to see if we could find a rooster. Sure enough, the dog would point, I would step ahead and a beautiful cackling rooster would explode out of the grass, his eyes staring at me, his wings shining in the sun.

What a sight! Those days are all gone. In the late 1970s the pheasants were all but gone. Now we have numerous predators, raccoons, coyotes, and red and grey foxes on the ground and all varieties of hawks and owls that have all but eliminated our game bird population. The younger generation will never experience the thrill of hunting a wild, ring-necked pheasant.

How did this happen? The pheasant population was studied and studied again. The biologists' conclusion was lost of habitat, farming changes, pesticides and predators. Well, I've been around pheasants all my life, over 65 years now, and I feel strongly that it was the increase in predators. The protection of hawks and owls by state and federal government during the 1960s coincided with the demise of the pheasant.

Then came the huge increase in four legged predators such as the coyote, fox, opossum, skunks, and the number one ground-nesting predator, the raccoon. I have seen huge increases in their populations. Another reason that ties in with the loss of the pheasant population is that the group of hunters that had been interested in hunting raccoon and fox has greatly decreased. I feel that, due to the lack of a reasonable fur price and the lack of young people entering recreational hunting, the predator population today exists in large numbers, and will for the foreseeable future.

The white-tailed deer is a beautiful animal when it is not in front of your new automobile. It used to be a novelty, a rarity, but it's become a dangerous nuisance in our densely populated areas. One big reason is their ability to adjust to the human population. We took their territory and now they are slowly taking it back. During the 1970s and '80s deer hunters from Niagara County would travel to their hunting camps to enjoy a week of male camaraderie. But that social event has slowly eroded away. Why should one drive fifty to one hundred miles to shoot a deer when we now have them in our backyards?

The number of archery hunters has continued to increase while the gun hunting continues to decline. It seems the younger generation of hunters prefer the quiet life of sitting in a tree stand, not only waiting to shoot a deer, but also to see the number of turkey, squirrels or song birds that fly inches from their faces. Who would have ever thought the deer would go from being the sacred cow to being a nuisance?

They've certainly become a danger to anyone driving a vehicle. Who is their predator? Look in the mirror and you'll see him; we are the last of the predators. There are no wolfs or mountain lions to reduce the herd, just man.

Waterfowl was another big hunting species. Large numbers of ducks would visit the wildlife areas in Orleans, Genesee, and Niagara Counties. During the 1970s and 80s there were clouds of Mallards, wood ducks, black ducks, teal, and other varieties to a lesser degree. What a sight at dusk to see large flights of them setting their wings. Then I started noticing fewer and fewer ducks. Why? The state said the numbers were high, but where were the ducks? After much discussion with other people in the know, I came to the conclusion that the wild ducks I had seen had changed their migration route to middle part of the state. There were always some ducks, but not the thousands I was used to seeing.

During the 1970s it was exciting to hear a flock of Canadian geese winging over the Tonawanda Wildlife Area. If I heard the "honk, honk" I would run to where I could see them. What a thrill. On many cool, crisp, fall days I would be in the

Tonawanda Wildlife Area and would hear that honk and see that distant "V" of the Canadian geese. What a great feeling to know the geese were back. But, by the early 1990s, Canadian geese had become a nuisance; they were nesting on every pond and golf course in New York State. And it wasn't just here; it was all over the United States. The Conservation Department had trapped and trimmed their wings so they could not fly and now we had too many geese. The state set a season in September to reduce the amount of local birds, which I agree with. So, we went from very few Canadian geese to overwhelming numbers of geese. A September season for the resident Canadian goose is now in effect to try to control their numbers.

Wild turkeys. Who would have ever thought that the turkey population would one day be in the thousands? Up to the mid-1970s there were no eastern wild turkeys. Thanks to the New York State Department of Environmental Conservation and their "trap and transfer" policy, there is now a spring and fall turkey-hunting season. Their population is constantly increasing due to the turkey's ability to adapt. I thought the turkey would never live in such close proximity to humans. I also feel that due to their size fewer predators attack them, unlike the pheasant and the ruffed grouse, which are easier for the hawks, fox, raccoons, and coyotes to attack. This is my own theory.

I cannot believe how the predator population has increased in the past 34 years. With the protection of hawks and owls the pheasants have disappeared and the raccoon, fox, skunk, and opossum are everywhere. Years ago it was rare to see raccoons in large numbers; now their population has exploded.

Ever since the early 1980's the coyote has populated all of New York State. It sounds primitive at night when I hear a coyote bark, like something from the old west. But I am sure the rabbit that just got killed does not appreciate it. The change in wildlife has gone from prey to predator. It is a rare sighting when I see a pheasant. I no longer see the bird dogs and rabbit hounds in back yards. Why keep a dog when the prey populations are so reduced?

I will end this chapter feeling very sentimental. During the early days of my career the prey were in large numbers...pheasant, rabbits, ducks. Then the predator's population increased to the point where we now have overwhelming numbers of raccoon, fox, and coyotes. The larger prey, like the Canadian geese and wild turkey, have all found their niche where they co-exist with the predators that inhabit western New York.

I would be a fool to predict the next thirty years.

Dick and wild turkeys

More Than Law Enforcement

I remember being a 14 year-old lad taking my New York State hunter safety class at the Erie County Fair. I did not know what to expect. I was part of a group of 25 young men waiting for the class to start and in walked two men in uniform. These two men were our instructors on game laws and hunter safety. Oh boy, did they impress me. I found out their job included not only catching bad guys, but also meeting with young people and talking to sportsmen's groups. Hey, I wanted to get good at this. What a great job, to be able to work in the outdoors and to wear a green uniform and carry a gun.

Now fast forward to October 1969. I had accomplished my dream of becoming a conservation officer. I was learning the job by accompanying the senior officers, checking deer, duck, and pheasant hunters. But, we also made time to visit the local hunter education classes where we could be seen in uniform as a friend and a person trying to help the sportsmen. I watched how the seasoned officers did their speaking and then put my own style and personality into what I felt was important.

I love props. I developed a law enforcement slide program of pictures that I would take of officers doing the varied aspects of the job. When we were on the Lake Erie boat I would have the camera ready, taking pictures of them checking fishing licenses and size limits. Working on cases involving endangered species, I would be there with my camera. Other officers from the Buffalo Region heard about my slide presentations and asked to borrow the slides.

This was great; I was on my way. But I needed more than just the slides. I needed large, blow-up pictures of the many activities of a conservation officer's duties. I went to my friends in the New York State Police photo lab, and asked if they could blow up some negatives into 16x20-inch photos. I was very pleased with their professionalism in assisting a fellow law enforcement agency. I used those pictures for 30 years, at career days and 6th grade field days, just to mention a few. They were excellent.

So, my props were growing in numbers, but I was still looking to develop more. I had started a collection of mounts before I became an officer but I needed a few more to complete my educational collection. These were not stuffed specimens; "stuffed" is what happens at Thanksgiving when you fill the turkey. These were specimens professionally mounted by a taxidermist.

Over the years I obtained many birds and animals that I thought could be used to tell a story. Some were killed along the highways while others were taken illegally. I used two different taxidermists in the area because they both did good work. But, my main source of mounted specimens came from the Buffalo Museum of Science. I would take in hawks, owls, herons and many other species that I would give or exchange for their taxidermy work. During the 1970's a new method of preserving small specimens was introduced into the art of taxidermy. It was called freeze-dried. For this method, the item is put into a controlled freezer, the mount is weighed and all the water removed. Using this method, the only thing artificial is the eyes.

My freeze-dried collection included a bullfrog, timber rattlesnake, and a fawn deer. The museum and I had a great working relationship for many years thanks to a man by the name of Arthur Clark. He was a professional in every way. The Buffalo Museum of Science can be proud they have such capable people working on their staff. With my freeze-dried collection to add to my slide and photo collection, I felt I was all set to go to the Cub Scouts, Boy Scouts and 4-H Clubs and show off my critters.

Then along came VHS videos, something more to add to my presentations. I taped programs on conservation law enforcement along with tapes on officer recruitment training. These I used at career days and other activities where students gathered to increase their knowledge of the outdoors.

Other times I would be expected to speak on specific subjects like what is legal to hunt coyotes with. I would study all the laws inside and out so I was prepared for any question or, as I called it, the WHAT IF question. There was always someone in crowd who would try to trip you up. But if you were prepared and knew your topic I found the audience always respected you.

My last prop was myself, in my green uniform, with my gun and my Stetson hat. That created questions about my job, uniform, and why did I carry a gun? And the big question, what does it take to become a conservation officer?

I always felt comfortable attending sportsmen's clubs. I enjoyed their company because I was a hunter, trapper and fisherman. I had done these activities and, with forty years experience, felt strongly that I could relate to them. I always felt that the way to get better at anything was just to do it. I enjoyed going to as many speaking engagements as possible. I felt this gave me name recognition. People began to see me as the community officer.

"Oh I know Dick Lang, He's the guy that came to the Hartland Conservation Club and talked about game laws."

Dick Lang (on right) with fellow officers and
"opportunities" clients, late 1990s

I was proud of the way I went about meeting the
public. Some officers did not like to go to sportsmen
clubs or schools; all they wanted to do was law
enforcement work. I always remembered the
impression those first two conservation officers made
on me at the hunter's safety class. I knew then, that if

my time came, I would try to teach a youngster how the conservation officer has a job to do when someone is breaking the law, but that he can also answer your questions to keep you out of trouble. And maybe, just maybe, someday my presentation will help a young person want to become a conservation officer.

2012 Retired Conservation Officers Golf Outing
Fred Evans, Tom Gouch, Dick Lang,
Dick Hannon, Dave Schultz, Tom O'Brien,
Allan Mills, Gary Bonseine

Things I Am Most Proud Of

I think we all get a sense of satisfaction when we know we've done a good job, whether in our professional career, a hobby, or just mowing the lawn. When I left my position as an environmental conservation officer, I had an inner satisfaction knowing I had done what I had set out to do, to be a respected, fair, knowledgeable officer and to have the same enthusiasm at the end of my career that I had when I started. Although I'm proud of my entire career, I've tried to list those achievements that, to me, are especially meaningful.

I love sports. Not only do I have a passion for hunting, fishing, and trapping but I also have a passion for competitive sports. I was the first conservation officer to participate in the New York State Police Olympics. At the age of thirty-two, I participated in freestyle wrestling, earning a silver medal. I then competed in track and field events such as the high jump, long jump, 400 meters, and the toughest-cop-alive competition. During that time I also competed in two more wrestling competitions. I was proud of the way I worked hard to earn those medals in track and field and wrestling.

Dick Lang, Tom Stoner, Terry Beck, Dan Sullivan, Dave Schultz, 1990s

As far as my professional career, after eleven years as a conservation officer I was honored to receive the Conservation Officer of the Year award in 1980, presented by the Eastern Chiefs.

In 1997 I was presented with the Lawman of the Year award by the Niagara County Police Chiefs and Magistrates Association. What a thrill to be chosen by my contemporaries in the same county where I lived and had made my career within law enforcement. To have my wife and two sons present made it all that much more special. Being recognized by the Niagara County Sportsmen's Federation on two different occasions as the Professional Employee of the Year was also very special.

When it came to new laws, I did have a direct effect on one of them. I was always looking out for the best interest of the sportsmen, and I disliked making a new law just to make a law, but sometimes it was beneficial. I was constantly suggesting the idea of extending the fall turkey season to the lake plains counties such as Niagara and Orleans. At first, the federation felt there would be heavy pressure on the birds. After three years of voicing my opinion, the federation supported the opportunity for our hunters to take a turkey in their local area and not harm the population. It has worked well, with no adverse affects on the turkey population.

I also spearheaded the stream improvements along 18-Mile Creek in the town of Newfane. For years I worked checking fishermen at 18-Mile Creek, wondering what could be done to improve the stream. I could envision improvements, but did not know how to get other people motivated to see what I saw. Then, due to the local town's violation of placing fill in the stream, we were able to assess the town a penalty, requiring them to do some environmental good. Groups from the Federal Government, the State Conservation Department, the County Soil and Water Agency, Environmental Planning, private clubs, and many others were interested but were not coordinated. Finally, a very organized person, Amy Fisk, from the county government got us all moving together and developed a plan. She helped us get the necessary permits and, within eight months of her taking on the task, the job was complete. A bulldozer and the work of many hands turned a stream that had been in trouble into a beautiful recreation area that the town of Newfane was very proud of and so was I.

In 1987 I was patrolling the Tonawanda Wildlife Area in the town of Royalton when I saw a new "For Sale" sign on a piece of property across from the wildlife area. I was concerned that if the wrong person purchased the property it could jeopardize hunting or shooting opportunities in the wildlife area. I called on the wildlife biologist, Dan Carroll, managing the area and he said the state had no money to purchase the property at that time. I insisted that I felt this was a critical piece of land that would tie in nicely with the management property presently owned. It was necessary to stop the possibility of homes being built in a migratory resting area. I then convinced the biologist, who I considered to be a friend, to visit the real estate office handling the property and see if we could put our own money down to hold the property until the state had time to come up with the balance.

Well, we did it, but it was close. While we were in his upstairs office finalizing the offer, a couple was downstairs considering a purchase offer of their own. The biologist and I each put up $100 of our own money and, with the private capital of other environmentally concerned people; the property was purchased and held for transfer to state holding. With some effort, good things really can happen.

The End Comes Too Fast

My career started to end long before it actually ended. The Department of Conservation did not appoint many officers and for my first ten years or so I was the rookie. I felt like I was still new and learning the job. I would look around a room of officers and they would all be ten to twenty years older than I was, with grey hair, weathered faces, and generally weighing over 200 pounds.

I stood six feet tall and weighed 160 pounds soaking wet. I had the height but I could hide behind a cattail real easy. At least that is what the duck hunters said. I was always in good health. I had a wrestling background, which I felt gave me confidence in many situations. I was quick and could run very fast, especially when I was chasing a violator.

By the time I reached the middle of my career, I was much more sure of myself. I felt I knew how to be at the right place at the right time to catch a violator. I knew in my heart that I was in the middle of my career, but it had come so suddenly. The fishing activities started in the spring, fishing and animal complaints in the summer, then hunting and fishing in the fall, and then the snowmobile, hunting and the many educational activities in the winter. Time went by in a blur.

Then I entered my last ten years and two things happened to remind me how fast time was going. It was the fall of 1994 and I was checking duck hunters in the Tonawanda Wildlife Area. I had my hip boots on and was headed for a group of four hunters who were hiding among the cattails, trying to imitate Mallards. I popped up through the cattails and identified myself as Conservation Officer, Dick Lang. As is most always the case, they knew of me and the oldest hunter piped up,

"Lang. I heard you retired."

Well, that was the first of many times people would say that to me. Then came the clincher.

It was March 1999, and I was accompanying Erie County Officer Ron Bosela on a complaint of illegal cement dumping along the banks of Lake Ontario. It was a cold, rainy Sunday when we arrived at the parking lot that overlooked the lake. Ron exited the green state car and proceeded to look over the bank. He stood a few minutes, looking over the situation, then made a turn and headed back towards our car. He was met by one of the summer residents who had come out to talk to him. I thought Ron was seeking information on who put the fill over the bank. After a short discussion he returned to our car. I asked,

"Well did you find out anything?"

"He says he does not know, but he said something odd."

"What's that, Ron?"

"Well, I asked him if he knew who dumped the cement. He said he did, but he wasn't going to tell me."

"Why not?"

"Well, he said Lang arrested him for the same thing a few years ago. A few minutes went by, then he said, 'I hear Lang is dead.' Well, I said, if he is dead, who is that sitting in that car?" Ron and I had a few laughs over that one as we drove over to the pier.

That just shows how fast you can go through a career. It seemed like just yesterday I was a rookie, then before I knew it I was in the middle of my career, and then a duck hunter heard I had retired. Then came the statement that really set me back, "I hear Lang is dead." No, thank goodness, I still had a few more years left to enjoy the best job in the world, a New York State Environmental Conservation Officer.

Nooooooo! I'm not ready to retire!

Retirement

How did it happen? How did thirty-four years of my life go by so fast? How did I get so old so fast?

Retirement is different for each conservation officer. For me, it was a very emotional time. I had submitted and pulled my retirement papers twice before finally submitting them for the last and final time. It was not an easy decision.

Retirement began as a state of mind for me. It started when I was in my late 50's. When I got together with other conservation officers, the conversation would often turn to, "When are you going to retire?"

"I don't know. I haven't thought about it."

I loved my job too much to retire. But, as I approached age 60 I started thinking about it and started going to all the retirement seminars. I also spent a lot of time talking about it with my wife, concerned about being able to afford it. Before I knew it, it was April of 2003 and I was 62. Now the thought of retirement was starting to get me excited. My mind was willing to continue fighting the good fight against the bad guys, but my body was starting to slip. I was having some serious health issues. I did not want to make a situation worse by being unable to perform my duties.

But knowing that still did not make it an easy decision. There was a lot of soul searching. On the one hand, why shouldn't I take it easy and do some of the fun things I enjoyed, like hunt, farm, travel, my wife's honey-do list? But would that be enough? For the past thirty-four years of my life, being a conservation officer was not just my job, it had been my passion. The job was made for me. If I wasn't a conservation officer, who would I be? What would my identity be? Of course, I would still coach wrestling and I wanted to get involved in town government. Maybe this was my chance. Back and forth my mind went.

Finally, I invited Bill Powell, Captain from Region 8, to my home to give me his opinion and any suggestions he might have. I valued Captain Powell's opinion greatly. Plus, he had retired about a year ahead of me, so had some experience with this phase of life. He listened to all my concerns and could feel the apprehension in my voice. He gave me a lot of valuable advice, but the words that had the greatest impact on me were: "Dick, you want to go out on top. If you continue to work, you will be setting yourself up for injury. Is that the way you want to leave? You don't want people to lose their respect for you or to pity you for your health issues. You are at the top of your game, everyone respects you. Don't lose that."

It made a lot of sense, and I knew he was right. But, truth be known, I was still filled with doubt, facing the unknown. There were no easy answers to the questions that continued to fill my head and kept me up at night: Who was I going to be? Will farming and town responsibilities take up enough of my time? I love my wife and family and my grandchildren are so much fun, but will that be enough? I had been behind the badge for so long…

Gretchen, Dick, and their grandchildren, 2004

There was no easy answer, but sometimes life answers for us. My health had gotten to the point where I could no longer perform the job with the energy, enthusiasm and commitment I had given it all my career. Bill was right, it was time to let it go. Now, nine years later, I can honestly say it was the right decision. I love my life now. As expected, I was and still am active with wrestling, I was town supervisor and met another whole range of acquaintances and friends, and I'm still in contact with other retired conservation officers. We get together periodically and reminisce, sharing experiences and old "war" stories.

And I have more time for my family, attending track meets, dance recitals and ball games with our seven grandchildren, and I finally have some time for my ever-patient wife, Gretchen. No, retirement was not an easy decision, but it was the right decision.

Gretchen and Dick, happily retired, 2010

Enjoying retirement with the family, celebrating Dick's induction into the Wrestling Hall of Fame, September, 2011.

What are those words?

There are some unusual words, abbreviations and shortcuts we use in Environmental Conservation. Here are some of them from my stories.

bush cop - slang for CO.

CO - conservation officer.

DEC - Department of Environmental Conservation.

deerjacker - illegal hunting (aid of a light) at night for deer.

ECO - environmental conservation officer.

ENCON (913) - ECO with car number.

gamie - slang for conversation officer (game warden).

jacking - illegal hunting (aid of a light) at night for deer, raccoons, fox, and coyotes.

pothole - a shallow water area, average depth less than 2 feet, usually under one acre in size.

sidearm - pistol.

snagging - catch a fish using a hook, bait or no bait; the hook penetrates the fish anywhere on the body, when the fisherman uses an exaggerated jerking motion of the pole.

spotlighting - illegal use of a spotlight at night while in possession of a firearm, crossbow, or bow.

tip up - signaling device for ice fishing to indicate that a fish has been caught.

Behind the Book

Books don't just happen. They not only require stories, they also require vision, knowledge, insight, and energy.

Dick and Gretchen's vision for this book started many years ago. Dick's notes over the years, his story-telling, his audiences, all have helped create **Behind the Badge**.

Author Dick Lang was born in Buffalo, New York. After graduating from high school, he enlisted in the U.S. Coast Guard. Following four years of service, he was honorably discharged in 1963. He was appointed a New York State Conservation officer in 1969 and retired in 2003. In 1980 he was New York's Conservation officer of the Year. He and his wife, Gretchen, reside in Lockport, New York. They have two sons and seven grandchildren.

Dick's email address is glang3@rochester.rr.com.

Illustrator Vic Thibault resides in Olcott Beach, N.Y. with his beautiful daughters, Ella and Emelia, and his wonderful wife, Sara. He teaches art in the Newfane Middle School, and owns and operates the Lake Ontario Art Factory, an airbrush and sign shop located on the shores of Lake Ontario in Olcott Beach. In addition to his love of art, Vic is an avid fisherman and lure maker.

In 1988, Dick came to Newfane to coach Vic's wrestling team. After college Vic became a member of Coach Lang's Wrestling team staff for 10 years. Though both have retired from coaching, they have remained good friends.

Coauthor Carol Miller is a retired microbiologist. After working in a very technical job for thirty-five years, she now enjoys the more creative endeavors of quilting, photography, and writing.

She and her husband, Mike, reside in Lockport and enjoy traveling in their spare time.

Carol's email address is missiecarol@cs.com.

Book designer and editor Mike Miller is a retired computer software developer turned artist, photographer, writer, and book designer. He and his wife, Carol, enjoy traveling, collecting more photos and stories to support their "habits"!

Mike has published articles and poetry in local and national newsletters, and his book *Acrostic Poetry and Some Prose* is available at Amazon.com.

Mike's email address is pubyourbook@gmail.com.

Made in the USA
Charleston, SC
04 November 2012